PRESUMED GUILTY

PRESUMED GUILTY

How the Jews Were Blamed
for the Death of Jesus

Peter J. Tomson

Translated by Janet Dyk

Fortress Press   Minneapolis

Published in cooperation with Meinema, an imprint of Boekencentrum Uitgeverij, Zoetermeer, Netherlands. Translated by Janet Dyk from the French, *L'affaire Jésus et les Juifs*, copyright © 2003 Cerf, Paris, France.

Unless otherwise noted, Scripture quotations are from the New Revised Standard Version Bible, copyright © 1989 by the Division of Christian Education of the National Council of the Churches of Christ in the USA, and are used by permission.

Cover design: Zan Ceeley
Cover art: *Ecco homo* by Honoré Daumier (1808–1879), Folkwang Museum, Essen, Germany. Photo © Erich Lessing / Art Resource, N.Y. Used by permission.
Interior design: Zan Ceeley and Beth Wright

Library of Congress Cataloging-in-Publication Data
Tomson, Peter J., 1948-
   [Affaire Jésus et les Juifs. English]
   Presumed guilty : how the Jews got blamed for the death of Jesus / Peter J. Tomson ; translated by Janet Dyk.
      p. cm.
   Includes index.
   ISBN 0-8006-3707-0 (pbk. : alk. paper)
   1. Jesus Christ—Passion—Role of Jews. 2. Jews in the New Testament. 3. Christianity and antisemitism—History. 4. Judaism (Christian theology)—History of doctrines.
I. Title.
   BT431.5.T6613 2005
   261.2'6'09—dc22
                                                    2004028682

09   08   07   06   05   1   2   3   4   5   6   7   8   9   10

Contents

Foreword

Publication of this book is sponsored by the Foundation for Scientific Research on Christian Literature on Jews and Judaism (Stichting Wetenschappelijk Onderzoek van Christelijke Literatuur over Joden en Jodendom), which is based in the Netherlands. The aim of the Foundation is to publish scholarly studies on the religious roots of anti-Semitism. Although much has been written on this subject in the past half-century, anti-Semitism has often been seen merely as a variant of racism. Racism most probably did play a role especially in the motivations behind the Spanish inquisition and the Nazis' hatred of the Jews. One of the lessons of the Shoah (the Holocaust), however, is that this racism could never have had such a catastrophic effect without the passive or active collaboration of many Christians. The reason behind that attitude must be sought in the negative portrayal of Jews within Christian circles. Although there would be sufficient reason to extend a similar project to include the Islamic world, the Foundation focuses on Christianity because of the course of recent European history.

To this end, the board of the Foundation has solicited the advice of Roman Catholic, Protestant, and Jewish experts. As a result, a study on the relationship to Judaism in the earliest collection of Christian texts, the New Testament, has been initiated. It was unanimously agreed to invite the Dutch Reformed theologian Dr. Peter J. Tomson to carry out this project. The Dutch edition having been well received, it was then published in English under the title 'If This Be from Heaven . . . ': Jesus and the New Testament Authors in Their Relationship to Judaism (Sheffield, England: Sheffield Academic Press, 2001), and other translations are being planned. The Foundation, however, especially desired to publish a more succinct account for a larger public, of which the present book is the English translation. In this case also, the Foundation aims to publish other translations, especially in Eastern European languages.

The board gratefully states its indebtedness to the many persons and institutions who by their contributions have made this project possible.

Dr. L. Robberechts, chairman
Dr. J. Wieberdink, secretary
D. te Winkel B.Sc., treasurer
Dr. T. Baarda
The Rev. S. Rozendal
Foundation for Scientific Research
on Christian Literature on Jews and Judaism
Kudelstaartseweg 148A
NL-1433 GN Kudelstaart
The Netherlands

Preface

What does the Jesus movement have to do with the Jews? Two answers can be given, one positive and one negative. The positive response is that Jesus and his first followers were Jews and remained Jews. The beginnings of Christianity must therefore be understood from the perspective of Judaism. The negative response is that Christians dissociated themselves from non-Christian Jews and began to view them as hostile competitors. They even came to assume that this was Jesus' intention. After this separation, to be a Christian appears to be synonymous with being anti-Jewish. For these two reasons we cannot discuss Jesus without involving the Jews.

The question of Jesus and the Jews has three aspects that must be distinguished:

1. The discussion of *Jesus' significance*. Deliberation about Jesus' meaning arose directly during his lifetime, came to an apex at his trial, and has never ceased since. It is a discussion among Jews but involves non-Jews as well, and it touches the core of Christianity. In order to understand anything at all about it we must have some understanding of the Judaism of that time. This aspect will recur in most chapters.

2. The actual *trial* and the *crucifixion*. The longest chapter at the center of this book is dedicated to this topic. Here all questions come together: Jesus' significance, his place in the Judaism of his day, the responsibility

of the Jewish and non-Jewish authorities, and the relationship between Jews and Christians. Moreover, the passion story is the main theme of the Gospels and is at the heart of the annual Easter celebration. The sign of the cross and the depiction of the crucified have become key elements in art and culture wherever Christianity has made its influence felt.

3. The general conflict between *Jews and Christians*. This aspect has unfortunately become dominant. Both Jews and non-Jews are accustomed to following a schematic way of thinking that has been present in the anti-Jewish church since the second century. In this schema, the discussion about Jesus' significance is overshadowed by the conflict between Jews and Christians. Jews are then by definition enemies of the gospel, and Christians are enemies of Judaism. All affinity between the gospel and Judaism is repressed, and Jesus' meaning can no longer be sought within his own Jewish context. This book has been written to help break through such a closed pattern of thinking.

Chapter 1 gives a bird's-eye view of how the Jesus movement developed into a conflict between Jews and Christians that continues to have effects today. Chapter 2 pursues the question as to what extent we can approach the "real" Jesus by means of available documents. Chapter 3 sketches the environment in which Jesus and his disciples lived and in which these documents emerged.

The real story then begins. Chapter 4 relates who Jesus was, how he acted, how he taught and treated his disciples, how he was viewed by others, and how he viewed himself. Chapter 5 presents Jesus' trial, the various standpoints concerning his meaning, the involvement of the authorities, the matter of the date in connection with the Jewish Passover, and the nature of the verdict. Chapter 6 is about the testimony of Jesus' disciples after Passover, new insights into his significance, the first churches in the Jewish homeland, and the spread of the new message among the non-Jews.

The last three chapters concern what happened thereafter. Chapter 7 discusses the decisive influence of the Jewish war with Rome. At that time the general conflict between Jews and Christians arose, and the first anti-Jewish churches emerged. Chapter 8 describes the New Testament writings in their divergent attitudes toward Jews and Judaism. Some writings are anti-Jewish; others are definitely not. Finally, chapter

9 contemplates how readers of the New Testament can deal with this diversity.

This book is addressed to the general reader. It takes both Jewish and Christian readers into account. Both are benefited by a distinction between Jesus' significance and the conflict between Jews and Christians. On the one hand, it is made clear how the Jews were made into enemies of Christianity. The Christian root of anti-Semitism is thus laid bare. On the other, space is created for a more correct evaluation of Jesus' meaning in his original, Jewish context. To the extent that the conflict between Jews and Christians is reduced to its human proportions, the discussion about Jesus' significance can gain in content.

Moreover, I have written this book for people who may not be at home with the Bible. I intend to appeal to reasonableness and to make the work comprehensible both to outsiders and to initiates. The question of Jesus and the Jews does not affect believers alone—although it is true that believers in particular are being addressed. The implications for believers are worked out in the final chapter.

Because in this book I aim for clarity and conciseness, those who desire further documentation and justification should consult my more extensive work, `If This Be from Heaven . . . ': Jesus and the New Testament Authors in Their Relationship to Judaism. I recommend this larger volume for those who use the present book as a resource in teaching.

To write a short book about a complex and emotionally charged issue is perilous, but it is also a challenge. The discussions that took place among the Foundation's board members and the procedure followed thereafter have strengthened me in the conviction that it is possible to write such a book. These discussions have helped to make clear how it should be done. It is essentially a probable account of observed happenings. The scholarly approach questions the degree of verisimilitude and emphasizes meticulousness in observation. In the more popular approach taken here, the issue is the comprehensibility of the account, and thus a simplification of the description is required. That is no small matter, as everyone involved in teaching realizes. The process is in itself not foreign to scholarship. Studying details and conceptualizing are two complementary functions. The scholar has truly understood a subject only when he or she is able to tell it to a child.

Verisimilitude is foremost; meticulousness remains implicit. Colleagues will assess many questions differently. That is part of the democratic process of scholarship. For the rest, I refer to my other book, though it only partially overlaps with the present one in theme. In the larger volume the historical analysis of the New Testament writings is predominant, while here the historical synthesis concerning Jesus' trial and his significance is the main focus.

I describe historically the question of Jesus and the Jews. I do not deny the theological significance; on the contrary, I assume that the dilemma "historical or theological" is false. In Chapter 2 I explain that it is not possible to be noncommittal when dealing with history. Even before we are aware of it, we are involved in the question of Jesus and the Jews. It is a *cause* that involves justice and injustice. *Who* committed the injustice and who did not—that is a historical question. What all of this could *mean* is a theological question inseparably bound to it.

The theological significance of Jesus is not to be sought outside of but within history. Jesus lived, preached, and believed among the Jews of his time. After his departure, his Jewish followers spread his message further. They were convinced of his unique significance. This conviction emerged during an eventful period of Jewish history. Their creed is then also a summary ("symbol") of his significance to the history of Israel or, better put, of "Israel and the nations." In Chapter 6 I show that the oldest Christian creeds are composed of Jewish concepts and beliefs.

Soon non-Jews were also drawn in. Under the circumstances of that time, this led to tensions and schisms. Even then, Jesus' significance continued to be seen in the context of the one history, however strife-torn. It is my conviction that the dilemma between a historical and a theological approach disappears when we seek the perennial origin of Christianity in its Jewish context.

With respect to form and style, I indicate relevant passages from the Bible at the end of paragraphs. In most cases these refer to the beginning of the passage involved; one must always read further! Reference is also made to pages within this volume where the theme being discussed is treated more extensively. For simplicity's sake, references to Jewish and other extrabiblical sources are given only by exception. In the survey of Jewish movements in Jesus' time in the appendix, a selection of sources is provided. Years are indicated by B.C.E. or C.E. (before or during the Christian or common era, respectively).

I have maintained the traditional designations "Old Testament" and "New Testament." In this I do not deny that the Jews were the first to read the Old Testament and that its message remains valid for Christians. There is much to be said for the terms "First" and "Second Testament." These avoid the impression that the first part is obsolete, and the difference between the Jewish and the Christian versions of the Bible remains clear. It is, however, equally possible to understand the terms "old" and "new" in that manner. That which is old is not necessarily diminished in value. A saying ascribed to Jesus himself praises *old* wine as being the best (Luke 5:39).

Thanks are due to those who directly contributed to the creation of this book: the board of the Foundation for Scientific Research on Christian Literature on Jews and Judaism and its secretary, Koos Wieberdink, for their sympathetic tenacity; Kees Waaldijk for his creative ideas; Tjitze Baarda and Rien de Jonge for their constructive criticism; Eric Ottenheijm for his professional advice. Having considered all advice, in the end I have gone my own way, and the shortcomings are my own. Special thanks once again to Janet Dyk for a creative and meticulous translation.

Finally, I am grateful to "Luke," the long-deceased author of the Third Gospel and the Acts of the Apostles. I have an ever-increasing admiration for the sensitivity with which he describes the history of Jesus and his followers in simple language, without cutting through complex knots. All three aspects of the Jesus cause come out clearly in his writings: the search for Jesus' significance, the trial itself, and the relationship between Christians and Jews. His two-part account is a model for scholars and a guideline for believers.

I dedicate this book to my children, and with them to all who will live the greater part of their lives in the twenty-first century. The question of Jesus and the Jews shall inevitably continue. The position chosen on this question is the personal responsibility of the reader. I hope this book will help to enable passion and study and to modestly prepare the way for understanding and open-heartedness between Jesus' followers and the Jews.

1

Jesus through the Ages

A Thirty-Year-Old Jewish Man

It all began with one man, a Jewish man about thirty years old. He was convinced that the kingdom of heaven was imminent and that he was sent to preach that good news and to put it into practice for the poor and the sick.

Many Jews believed him. In what he did and said they recognized the ancient prophets' words of hope. They believed that he was the promised *Messiah*, the "Anointed One." Anointed as a king at his coronation, the Messiah would come to bring a kingdom of peace and justice. Others were not so sure. Jesus' message was appealing and encouraging, and they admired his work among the poor and the ill—but had the messianic kingdom really dawned? Were wars and injustice banished? There were yet others who thought that he was dangerous, an agitator who deluded the people with attractive sermons about a golden future. The last group were successful in having the Romans get rid of him.

His death was not the end. Jesus' cause persisted. Several of his followers had seen him. He was "raised from the dead." They had read about this in the ancient writings of the prophets, about which he himself had spoken so frequently. The coming of God's kingdom was not to be impeded.

Their master's death and resurrection were not unrelated to this but were its secret. Had he not sacrificed his life for God's kingdom; was his blood not shed for all? They read more in the words of the prophets. Not only was he raised from the dead, but he also sat at God's right hand in heaven. From there he would soon return upon the clouds with tens of thousands of angels to judge the nations righteously.

In joyful anticipation, Jesus' disciples took over his tasks. During his lifetime, Jesus had already sent them forth to preach the good news to the poor and to heal the sick. They now carried this on. They preached everywhere in the Jewish homeland, including to the non-Jews who lived there and who often attended the synagogue. Jesus' followers brought the good news to other countries as well—to Syria, Asia Minor (modern-day Turkey), Greece, and Italy. They traversed the whole inhabited world, even as far as Egypt and India, according to later reports.

Thus everywhere *churches* emerged, congregations of Jesus. To a large extent these resembled synagogues. The members congregated on Saturday or Sunday, sang songs of praise, faithfully read aloud from the Bible, and listened to someone who had something to say about it. On other days they cared for the rest of community life—civic matters such as marriages, disputes, and relief for the needy. There was one important difference: the churches not only read from Moses and the prophets but also retold the words and deeds of Jesus as his disciples remembered them. In many synagogues, disagreements arose on this topic. (Luke 4:16; Acts 13:15; 20:7)

By now we have progressed to the 40s and 50s of the first century. The members of many churches began to call themselves "Christians." *Christos* is the Greek translation of "Messiah," the "Anointed One," about whom the Psalmist and the prophets wrote. This title was applied to Jesus, and from that his followers' new name, "Christian," originated. Soon all of Jesus' followers, both Jews and non-Jews, were thus designated. Only later, when the churches began to be constituted solely of non-Jews, did the term "Christian" become equivalent to "non-Jew." (Acts 11:26)

Up to that point, customarily there were both Jews and non-Jews in the churches. In some places, such as in the Jewish homeland, the Jews formed a majority; elsewhere they were a minority. The churches were comprised of Jews and non-Jews—"Jews and Greeks," as they were commonly called. This combination at times caused difficulties, but certainly not always.

The mealtime, for example, could present problems. Some Jews were afraid that non-Jews never would be totally free of idolatry as long as they had not converted fully to Judaism. While eating together, the Jews would thus be implicated in idolatry. On the other hand, some non-Jews had no patience with Jewish dietary regulations. The Jewish religion happens to express itself in certain rules such as the prohibition of eating meat not properly slaughtered or of eating certain animals. "Those animals have *mazel!*" as the Jewish joke goes (*mazel* means "random fate" or "luck"). For such practical problems, practical solutions can be found if parties trust one another. That has been the case throughout the ages.

The Anti-Jewish Church

Distrust won out. The blame for this lay neither entirely with the non-Jews nor with the Jews. For a large part, it lay in the political whirlpool into which they were both sucked. In 66 c.e. radical elements in the Jewish homeland began a war with Rome. All relationships were put on edge. Existing tensions among the Jews themselves suddenly changed into mortal enmity. The same happened to relationships between Jews and non-Jews. Both in the Jewish homeland and elsewhere violence broke out between Jews and non-Jews. This, too, has occurred throughout the ages. In Bosnia, Roman Catholic, Eastern Orthodox, and Muslim citizens had been living side by side for centuries. The war that broke out in 1992 caused a neighbor or brother-in-law suddenly to be a "Croatian," "Serbian," or "Muslim"—a mortal enemy in this hostile atmosphere.

When in 70 c.e. the war against Rome ended with the destruction of the temple in Jerusalem, society had been plowed up like a battlefield. Jews and non-Jews no longer trusted one another; those with divergent beliefs were avoided by both. Eating together became a problem, praying together often impossible. Thereafter churches and synagogues went their separate ways. In the synagogues, especially in the Jewish homeland, there arose a tendency to exclude followers of Jesus from the community. As time passed, things did not improve. In 132–135 c.e. a second revolt against Rome blazed, ending in an even greater disaster for the Jews. The breach with Jesus' followers was irreparable. Jews were no longer allowed to dwell in Jerusalem, and the church there had non-Jewish bishops from then on.

In the second and third centuries, mainstream Christianity became an exclusively non-Jewish movement. Christian theologians began to react against the Jews and argued that the Jewish interpretation of Moses and the prophets had been wrong from the beginning. Judaism came to be viewed as the major rival. The consciousness of the Jewish origin of many customs and beliefs was repressed. In such ways, anti-Jewish thinking emerged within the church. The Jews who were already skeptical of Christianity or who rejected it felt themselves even more threatened as anti-Jewish thinking gained in influence. The enmity was mutual.

Not that Christianity was a unity. Each of various churches transmitted the story of Jesus in its own manner. Gradually the need for fixed guidelines arose. A number of churches found an anchor in the tradition of the apostles; they called themselves "apostolic." Just as the apostles had done, they continued to read aloud from Moses and the prophets, although they now interpreted these in an anti-Jewish manner. Other groups went further and dispensed completely with Moses and the prophets. The God of the Old Testament had created the earth as a vale of tears from which Jesus as the heavenly Savior had come to liberate humankind. Such groups were called *Gnostics* and eventually came to be regarded by the dominant churches as "heretics." The apostolic churches contested such ideas fiercely.

During that time, various types of Jewish churches emerged that belonged neither to the Judaism of the rabbis nor to the "apostolic" churches of the non-Jews. Naturally, they continued to read aloud from Moses and the prophets, and they told the story of Jesus in their own manner. The bishops of the "apostolic" churches condemned these because they kept the law of Moses. They lived in a no-man's-land.

Meanwhile Christian writers had committed Jesus' life and teachings to writing. Such a document is called a *Gospel*. Several of these were in circulation. *Epistles* (letters) written by apostles to their churches were also collected here and there. In the meetings, these writings began to be read aloud alongside Moses and the prophets. They expressed that which bound the congregation together in its competitive struggle. In some of the texts the enmity between Jews and Christians is clearly delineated. During the second century, the collection emerged that came to be designated the *New Testament*. Alongside it, the books of Moses and the prophets continued to be read in the worship service. The latter were together now called the *Old Testament*. The Christian Bible was thus born amidst rivalry with the Jews. (Colossians 4:16; 2 Peter 3:15)

The ensuing centuries brought harsh times for the churches. Conservative Romans were worried by the fact that the new religion began to spread among the upper levels of society. Evil intent and fear led at times to persecutions, which could be particularly vicious if the emperor himself stood behind them, as happened especially during the third century. The Jews were better off. On the basis of ancient privileges they had as yet a recognized position within the Roman Empire.

At the beginning of the fourth century, the tide changed. The ruling emperor, Constantine, converted to Christianity and began to support it more or less officially. It became the most powerful religion in the empire. In contrast, the situation of the Jews deteriorated rapidly. Imperial laws were decreed that benefited the Christians, made association with the Jews difficult, and deprived the Jews of several privileges. Thus Christianity emerged from antiquity. From that point on, a triumphal, anti-Jewish church made its appearance as the advocate of the Jesus movement.

Middle Ages, Reformation, Revolution

In medieval Europe, the position of the Jews was unstable, dependent on the ambivalent attitude of Christians. On the one hand, the most prominent leaders, who now resided in Rome, thought that the Jews should not be totally suppressed. Even though the supposed Jewish infidels had rejected and killed Jesus, they were in the end still God's chosen people. On the other hand, nowhere did the Jews have fixed rights, and they were banished first from one country and then from another.

Such ambiguous politics could not, of course, be explained to the people. Whenever there was misfortune, the Jews were held responsible. The Crusades aimed at the "liberation" of the Holy Land from the Muslims, but led first to tens of thousands of Jewish victims. When the plague broke out, the Jews were blamed. When they applied themselves to banking—

a vocation prohibited by the church to its members—the Jews were seen as extortioners. Theological condemnations led to massive burnings of the Talmud. In this climate, the anti-Jewish accents in the Gospels had a powerful influence.

The *Reformation* of the sixteenth century had a certain favorable effect for the Jews. Its regional and national character caused the power of the church to fragment. A certain degree of tolerance emerged in republics such as Holland. Further, the desire for Bible translations led to interest in biblical Hebrew and to contact with rabbis. There was a clear connection here to humanism, the new interest in humanity and culture. It involved as well an interest in Greek, the language in which the New Testament was written. At that time, humanism did not mean atheism. One was a "Christian humanist" and attempted to follow Jesus by loving God above all and one's neighbor as oneself. On the other hand, this did not entail a general sympathy toward the Jews. Only seldom were Jews recognized as "neighbors." When things went badly, Martin Luther also could resort to anti-Jewish language. The ambiguous position of the Jews was not over. (Mark 12:29)

The *revolutions* that broke out in the United States of America and in France at the end of the eighteenth century—and later in other lands— were a mixed blessing as well. The governmental power of the church was permanently broken, and that meant an improvement for the Jews. Civil equality brought emancipation, and many Jews found their way to the top of society. At the same time, however, in France and other European countries, *all* religions were restricted, including the Jewish religion. The interests of the nation were primary. Time would reveal that anti-Jewish sentiments were in no way banished. In the United States, in contrast, equality meant freedom of religion, and this was an ideal climate for Judaism. In the twentieth century, the greatest Jewish community in the world was to emerge there.

During the same period, the question of Jesus was given a new turn by *historical research.* Emancipation from clerical authority meant that religions, too, came to be explained historically. Attempts were made to surpass tradition and distortion to capture the "historical Jesus." Few, however, understood that he must be sought in his own Jewish context. Scholarly research followed the trends of nineteenth century society, and only Jewish scholars had a real interest in Judaism. Nonetheless, the discovery of forgotten Jewish texts led to a correction of the image of early Judaism. Through this it would become possible to understand Jesus again as a Jew among the Jews.

The Twentieth Century

The twentieth century leaves no room for superficial optimism. The ideologies that emerged in the nineteenth century flourished. In the wake of the revolution, these purely political philosophies pursued a nonreligious structure of society. They gave rise, however, to unprecedentedly violent forms of government. Once again, Jews were among the first victims. Not only was this an injustice, but it also gave reason for some serious thought. Ideologies against religion were born out of the battle, but they showed themselves to be inseparably related to it. Seen from a distance, there were apparently multiple connections to the question of Jesus and the Jews.

The beginning of the century witnessed extreme nationalism. Externally this led to an unparalleled development of European colonialism in Africa and Asia. Internally it was accompanied by fear of and hate for anything unfamiliar, in particular the Jews. *Anti-Semitism* became popular in France and Germany. A number of Jews chose their own ideological solution: *Zionism*, the pursuit of a Jewish national state. In 1914 it became apparent what nationalism was capable of. Blinded by pride and fear, the "civilized" world plunged itself into a World War. Christians, Jews, socialists, and humanists finished each other off by the millions. In a deeply sobering manner, church and culture dedicated themselves to the bloody worship of the fatherland.

In comparison to their conditions under the czars, initially the 1917 communist revolution in Russia was an improvement for the Jews. Strict anti-religious politics, however, made the exercise of religion, including Judaism, extremely difficult. Stalin's violent regime even had an overt anti-Semitic accent to it. Italian fascism (1919) produced comparatively little damage. In contrast, German nationalism (1919) made the campaign against the Jews a spearhead of its program.

Hitler's takeover in 1933 led directly into World War II and to a new nadir in the history of humankind. Half of European Jewry was industrially disposed of as a noxious race. After the war, the world hesitatingly allowed what had happened to register. Such systematic mass murder was a shocking innovation—and that in a country that counted itself as a cradle of culture! In the countries occupied by the Germans, only a small minority had assisted the Jews. The majority had kept silent or collaborated. In hindsight, many recognized Christianity's negative image of the Jews to be behind this.

A large portion of surviving Jews left for Palestine. The United Nations made a plan of partition. When the Arabic countries did not acknowledge this, the Jews proclaimed the founding of the State of Israel in 1948. The world was saddled with a new problem: the Israeli-Arab conflict. Again the struggle was expressed on an ideological plane. Arab nationalism saw Zionism as a fundamental threat. These certainly were, however, not unrelated to religion. For Jews around the world, observant or otherwise, Israel was henceforth the basis of their existence. Muslims were divided between a realistic acceptance of the Jewish state and "pan-Islamic" resistance. Christians, especially in the West, could no longer ignore Judaism. "Israel" was back on the world stage.

This realization began to penetrate theology. According to some, ever since the New Testament, anti-Jewish thinking had been inseparably bound to the confession of Jesus as Messiah. Others emphasized the Jewish origins of Christianity. They found support in ancient Jewish texts, such as the Talmud, and even more clearly in the Dead Sea Scrolls (1947). The track that was discovered in the nineteenth century led to new insights into the question of Jesus and the Jews.

The second half of the century witnessed also the process of decolonialization. The peoples of Africa, Asia, and South America began to appear on the world stage in the United Nations (1948). In the same year the World Council of Churches recognized the share these peoples have in the Jesus cause. By the end of the century this share has proved to be indispensable to its continuation.

We might well wonder what the new millennium will bring. The violent and anti-Jewish potential of Christianity is already known. Twentieth-century ideologies have done no better. Fascism and national socialism have been beaten; communism has collapsed under inner contradictions. A new nationalism offers footing to threatened ethnic groups and is often accompanied by bloody religious fanaticism. Local wars demand millions of victims on a worldwide scale. Neo-capitalism flourishes in a global economy that makes the rich richer and the poor ever poorer.

While religions and ideologies churn, what does the story of that one man with whom it all began signify? To find an answer we must learn to see him anew in his own time: a Jewish man who believed that he had the mission of proclaiming to the rejected of the earth that God's reign of justice and love is at hand.

2

The Quest for the "Real" Jesus

One man through the ages appeals to the imagination. In such a case it is unavoidable that the imagination makes its own contribution. Does not each age, each culture create its own image of Jesus? Since the nineteenth century we can no longer uncritically continue to do so. We have become aware of the difference between self-made images and Jesus as he must have been in his own time.

The shift is related to a new awareness that emerged at the beginning of the nineteenth century, namely, historical consciousness. Humans are historical beings. All that we do, say, and think—and even what we believe—is in one way or another to be understood in relation to our history. The sequence in time is determinative. Things that precede lead to those that follow; that which is younger is born from that which is older. Likewise, the image of Jesus as the Second Person of the divine Trinity is irrefutably later than that of the carpenter from Nazareth. That is why the latter has historical priority. (Mark 6:3)

This is not to say that what comes later is of no value. Someone's significance can later supersede his historical circumstances. Insight into this can only come in due time. Then indeed the "imagination" can contribute: long-cherished images are linked to this one person. Something of the sort has happened with Jesus. From being a historical person, he has become the main theme in an elaborate doctrine of faith. An essential question presents itself: who is the "real" Jesus?

The Historical Jesus or the Christ of Faith?

This question of the historical Jesus or the Christ of faith has dominated nineteenth- and twentieth-century theology. It is a profound dilemma. Many were convinced that historical research could never reach the "real" Jesus; that can be done by faith alone. Others countered that an approach through faith is not open to historical reality, while that is where the "real" Jesus must be sought. Behind these lies a question with which many still struggle: what does Christian faith have to do with historical reality?

Adherents of the historical approach began searching for the *"historical Jesus,"* Jesus in his original surroundings. Their endeavors were less than successful, because they viewed Judaism as an outmoded, inferior religion. The "religious genius" of the carpenter from Nazareth must tower far above that. He must, therefore, have drawn from other spiritual sources— but what these were remained a question. What Jesus initiated, however, would have been carried through by *Paul.* Paul abolished the Jewish law and placed at the center a Greek-tinted *faith in Christ.* Thus he became the second and true founder of Christianity as a genuinely universal religion. This approach assumed a contrast between Jesus and Paul. It also showed a preference for a Greek context.

Many believers protested against this argumentation. For them Jesus was not merely a Jewish carpenter who through a complicated procedure was made into the main figure of Christianity. He must have been the promised, divine Christ from the very beginning, the Savior of whom Moses and the prophets had spoken. Jesus came to reveal God's judgment and grace and by his death to atone for human sin. Only faith in him can bring eternal salvation. With this insight Paul completed the work of Christ. Because the historical approach had no eye for such matters, it was rejected as damaging to faith.

Both approaches excluded each other. Either one sought the historical Jesus and lost faith in Christ, or one entrusted oneself to the Christ of faith and disregarded historical reality. This was not only an unnatural partition of reality; it was also a tragic dilemma that split churches, anathematized universities, and caused multitudes to lose their faith.

Nonetheless, at the end of the twentieth century a solution began to emerge. This came about by simultaneously taking note of another problem that is somewhat similar and that arose at the same time. Long neglected, it has only recently received general attention. This is the question of Jesus' relationship to Judaism.

As already noted, historians were not too successful at placing Jesus in his original surroundings because they saw Judaism as an outmoded religion. Their own Christian tradition no doubt played a significant role in this. Whatever the outcome, the Christian faith must have emerged somewhere else than from Judaism. Thus they assumed in fact an unbridgeable gap between Judaism and Christianity. Purely historically, this is an improbable and unlikely rendering of reality. It is therefore likely that there is a relation here to the unnatural gap between historical reality and Christian faith. Could the opposition of faith and history have been caused by attempts to explain the emergence of Christianity as the antithesis to Judaism?

We can find confirmation of this surmise by simply assuming the opposite. By viewing Jesus and his first followers in a positive relationship to Judaism, the connection between Christian faith and historical reality becomes at once much clearer. We can then take Jesus' own Jewish faith as a point of departure. By extension, we can well understand the creed in which his first, Jewish followers summarized his significance. It is then also no longer necessary to assume an antithesis between Jesus and Paul. Within the Jewish history of that time, we are concerned with one and the same Jesus—the *historical* Jesus and his significance for the *faith* of his first followers.

Involvement in History

The gap between faith and historical reality is also related to our own *involvement* in the issue. The approach through faith places personal involvement first. For this reason it is often dismissed as "subjective." In contrast, the historical approach tries to be "objective" and minimizes personal involvement. This concept of historiography, called "positivist," arose in the second half of the nineteenth century. During the twentieth century it came under heavy criticism.

One of the reasons for the criticism is that the past century has produced such an unprecedented amount of war and violence. Many acquired an aversion to history, the more so since it had been glorified during the nineteenth century. Such feelings were particularly intense directly after the First and Second World Wars. This helps to explain the tendency to push aside disappointedly the historical approach and its presumed objectivity. A new line of thought emerged, dialectical theology, in which actual history and subjective involvement are less important. Instead, the "objectivity" of revelation is at the center.

At the beginning of the twenty-first century, more than ever we live "in history." Daily world events are documented many times over; the past is massively present. All this historical reality can even seem surrealistic. A new generation grows up with the question: is what we call "history" merely one of the virtual or imaginary realities? Is there truth in our history? In this book, we assume confidently the affirmative: it must be about here and now, truth and falsehood, justice and injustice, wrongs and rights. Commitment is unavoidable: readers themselves are totally involved.

"Historical reality" is not an object one can study and explain with no strings attached. One who is not personally involved in history will never study it. Involvement is the engine of historiography. Without indignation at the role of oppression by Christians or others in positions of power, without compassion for other people, no new impulses in historiography would emerge. Indignation and compassion are, however, not enough. Historiographers must be self-critically aware of their own involvement. Involvement itself is not the rudder of historiography. It must be continually and critically adjusted to what is encountered in reality, to what is observed and read.

A Cause Involving Justice and Injustice

We are already involved—through history itself. A responsible person cannot be occupied with the question of Jesus and the Jews without becoming involved. Innumerable victims have been claimed, and much injustice has been done. One who backs away from history or who approaches history as a lifeless object abandons the victims to their unfair lot. The history of Jesus and the Jews is a cause involving justice and injustice.

As in all lawsuits, both sides must be heard. It is not simply justice versus injustice. There is not just one huge guilty party, Christianity. The Jews are not merely victims. Christians and Jews, each in their own way, are involved in the Jesus cause.

In the traditional Christian viewpoint, "the Jews"—all Jews—are guilty of the execution of Jesus. This is a schematic way of viewing the matter in which the case of Jesus is made into a case against the Jews. The Jews are then enemies of Jesus and Christianity, and Jesus and his followers are placed opposite to Judaism. This anti-Jewish standpoint arose at the end of the first century and became dominant in the fourth century. It has caused an indescribable amount of suffering among the Jews, especially in Europe. This point of view still continues to have its effect, but since World War II it has been progressively abandoned. Thus room has been made for the question as to who actually were the guilty ones in the case of Jesus.

A just approach demands that a distinction be made between the case of Jesus itself and the case against the Jews. Jesus was executed by the Romans at the insistence of Jewish authorities. Among Jesus' first followers there were victims resulting from initiatives from the Jewish side. This belongs to the broader question of Jesus' significance. It touches the core of Christianity, and it is difficult to provide a final answer. The point is, however, that there were Jewish leaders who felt they must give that answer. Which leaders they were and what their motives were are what the research into the question of Jesus is about.

At the same time, the recognition of Christian guilt toward the Jews must not lead to a general condemnation of Christianity. Though understandable, it would be an overreaction. That approach is equally schematic and does nothing to clarify the question of Jesus. What is needed is to differentiate on which points and to what extent Christians and their writings are worthy of blame. Why should they all be so in each case? It is important as well to underscore where the Christian tradition is not culpable—where Christians in good conscience can stand for their faith.

This book is particularly about the question of Jesus itself—not about the whole history of the Christian cause against the Jews. Its beginning, however, is of essential importance. The most important document in the question of Jesus, therefore, is the New Testament. This is also the main Christian document. The entire existence of the church and of Christianity is dependent upon it. In the traditional point of view, the New Testament serves as justification of the Christian cause against the Jews. The big question is, to what extent is this correct? There is but one way to find an answer—by careful and unprejudiced reading and rereading.

We must learn to distinguish between the question of Jesus and the case against the Jews *within* the New Testament. In which portions does the original Jesus movement appear to be reasonably purely recorded? In which portions does the later conflict with the Jews dominate? This research puts believing Christians to the test. What must they do if it becomes apparent that anti-Jewish accents are present not only in later Christian writings but also in the New Testament itself? Is that possible within the Holy Scriptures? How this test could be dealt with is discussed below, in the final chapter.

A choice must be made. Either we take the question of justice and injustice seriously and include the New Testament in our research, or we keep the New Testament out of range. In the latter case the question of justice and injustice cannot be fully addressed. One who chooses that option would do better to lay this book aside. The aim here is, in all simplicity, to examine thoroughly the question of Jesus and the Jews and to include the entire New Testament. There is no alternative; it is our most important source.

Sources and Interpretations

I have stated that the most simple approach is to assume a positive relationship between Jesus and Judaism. How should we conceive of this? Which form of Judaism did Jesus encounter in his day? What did he himself consider positive? Who can be a judge in this matter? Is there objective footing?

There is such, and becoming aware of this is one of the achievements of modern times. Our footing lies in the *historical sources*, documents in which the reality of Jesus' time is recorded. They contain what of his reality has come down to us. It is not essential here whether a certain image of Jesus or of Judaism appeals to us or not. What is determinant is whether it corresponds to the sources. To the extent that it does, it is "real."

These sources cannot in themselves be called objective footing. *Which* sources are important? Scholars disagree on this point. They agree even less about what is to be read in these sources. Scholars are human; whether they like it or not, they are involved. On the basis of their own insights, they select and interpret the sources they consider to be valuable. If they want to understand their task in a truly scientific manner, they should remain self-critical and delineate points of discussion and uncertainty. There is no escaping this: even those who believe that the Bible is literally the Word of God do not possess a direct revelation concerning the historical reality of Jesus. Approaching historical reality remains the result of human effort.

Many, therefore, are disappointed and abandon the quest for the real Jesus. Is not our knowledge, after all, limited? Understandable as this position may be, it reveals a lack of realism. Our knowledge is indeed limited, but it is not thereby unreal. Like all reasonable knowledge, historical knowledge is an *approximation* of reality. What "truly" happened is reconstructed on the basis of observations and experiences. No more than that, but also no less. This is as true of the report of a traffic accident or of a physics experiment as of a historical process. We make historical reconstructions on the basis of what we observe in the sources.

Even then our knowledge remains limited; *we* are the ones who select and interpret. The danger is that we go around in a circle: we consider certain sources to be important because we are familiar with them, but we are acquainted with them because we consider them to be important. Thus it is tempting to restrict ourselves to the New Testament as the single source of the reality concerning Jesus. After all, we know this source well: we consider it important! The danger is even more acute vis-à-vis the question of Jesus and the Jews. How can we escape from this closed circle? We can do so by involving other sources and broadening our foothold. New discoveries and curiosity concerning sources as yet unexploited are essential in this.

New discoveries appeal to the imagination. Herein lies a danger as well: romantic exaggeration. A new discovery is too quickly seen as "the definitive revelation" after centuries of ignorance, as can be observed in the ado about the Dead Sea Scrolls. But new discoveries can only add to already available information, not replace it. There is no direct access, no instant knowledge. Who Jesus really was in his time can only be reconstructed by patient puzzling with the available sources, both old, familiar ones and newly discovered ones.

Ancient Jewish Writings

To prevent going around in circles when reading the New Testament, we must consult other sources. Which should these be? A general guideline would seem obvious. The issue is the relationship of Jesus and his followers to Judaism. That gives *ancient Jewish sources* priority. Jesus' attitude toward Judaism must first and foremost be tested by comparing the New Testament with ancient Jewish writings.

Formerly the historical approach preferred to concentrate on the *Greek* context of early Christianity, often to the exclusion of Jewish texts. This position is no longer tenable. Because the Jewish texts that interest us are themselves only to be understood within the context of the ancient world, information supplied by Greek and Roman writers is of great consequence. Indirectly, these are therefore also significant for us, but in this book I hardly touch upon them. For this investigation, ancient Jewish texts require primary attention.

Of chief importance are the scrolls discovered since 1947 at *Qumran* near the Dead Sea. Their importance is due, first, to their antiquity. These Hebrew texts are at least as old as the writings of the New Testament— some clearly much older. Second, they provide inside information about a previously unknown Jewish manner of thinking and living. They apparently belonged to the movement of the Essenes. The Essenes were already known from ancient sources, but this information was from the outside. Third, the scrolls make it possible to achieve a much more precise reconstruction of first-century Judaism as a whole. Our footing in the world of Jesus' time is thus considerably increased. Through this it is possible to utilize more effectively the information from already long-known Jewish sources.

Among the previously known Jewish sources, the *rabbinic literature* is noteworthy. Like the Qumran scrolls, it is for a large part cast in Hebrew. Rabbinic texts contain many elements that reveal essential affinity to the New Testament and are therefore highly significant. These will be discussed in the following chapter.

Not to be neglected are the ancient Jewish texts written in Greek, that is, the *Hellenistic-Jewish writings*. There are a number of misconceptions concerning these. In comparison to the "orthodox" rabbis, these are often assumed to contain a watered-down form of Judaism. While traditional Jewish scholars viewed this as negative, Christians viewed it as positive, thinking that "nonorthodox" Judaism in itself would be closer to Christianity. Both overlooked the fact of how varied the Judaism of the first century was. It included a full-blown Jewish culture that expressed itself in Greek. Aside from a couple of exceptions, this has disappeared. The few Greek-Jewish writings that have survived are crucial to the understanding of the New Testament.

A number of other ancient Jewish texts have been rescued from oblivion by creative scholars. This, too, was a result of the new historical interest of the nineteenth century. Churches in countries such as Ethiopia, Syria, and Armenia appeared to have preserved all sorts of writings in which ancient Jewish texts are incorporated. Most of these contained retellings of the Bible and visions concerning the future (the latter are related to the biblical book of Daniel, but contain many details hitherto unknown). An important example is *1 Enoch*, an apocalypse preserved in Ethiopia.

The Gospels

The primary documents for the question of Jesus are the Gospels. There are literally whole libraries written about them. My interest here is the proximity to the surroundings of Jesus himself that is reflected in them.

The New Testament contains four different Gospels. There must have been many more, perhaps even in forms quite different to what we now know. We are aware of this because of the so-called *Gospel of Thomas* found in 1945 in Egypt in the midst of an old collection of books. It consists only of sayings of Jesus loosely connected by brief narrative phrases. The

Gospel of Thomas probably was given its final form at the end of the second century. The gap in time makes one suspect remoteness to Jesus environment. Indeed there is quite a distance in mentality from what we encounter in the oldest Gospels, and we are reminded of the Gnostic groups that opposed the "apostolic" tradition in the second century. Nonetheless, the Gospel of Thomas contains some valuable ancient versions of Jesus' words.

The four biblical Gospels are the oldest known to us. The first three concur strongly in language and atmosphere, even in the portions that do not appear in all three of them. They must, therefore, originate from the same broad tradition. The impression is given that they go back to an oral tradition of Jesus' words and deeds. Comparison with ancient Jewish writings confirms that they reflect Jesus' own setting. Further, in these Gospels, Peter, in spite of all of his shortcomings, counts as the most important disciple. Elsewhere in the New Testament, he is presented as the leader of the church in Jerusalem. The first three Gospels thus stem from the tradition of Jesus' disciples where Peter plays a major role. (pp. 30, 78)

Of these three Gospels, *Mark* is the oldest. It was written perhaps during or just after the war with Rome. Here and there it appears to have been transcribed directly from oral tradition. This text was subsequently taken as starting point by the authors of *Matthew* and *Luke*. Each added large portions of Jesus' teachings. For this they must also have drawn partially from a *collection of the sayings of Jesus*, manuscripts of which are no longer known. The reworking of Mark must have emerged in the generation following the war when the relation of Jesus' followers to the Jews had become strained. Various effects of this are noticeable in the texts.

Attributing the Gospels to the evangelists Matthew, Mark, and Luke is a later development. The historical value of this differs per case. For convenience, we speak simply of "Matthew," "Mark," and "Luke."

The fourth biblical Gospel, that of *John*, has its own history, as is apparent even from its own peculiar language and style. Here again the name of the writer was added later. The Gospel appears to be more remote from Jesus' disciples than are the first three. Moreover, it belongs to the youngest texts of the New Testament. Tension with the Jews is deposited here in the strongest form.

For whom were the Gospels intended? Many characteristics indicate that all of the biblical Gospels in their present form were written for non-Jewish readers. But, just as clearly, use is made of what was transmitted by Jewish Christians. From this we cannot as yet make deductions as to the attitude toward the Jews. One can write for non-Jews while being positive toward Jews. One can also use Jewish-Christian traditions and yet treat Jews negatively. In the New Testament, both are to be found.

An essential question, finally, is how we can use the Gospels for our historical reconstruction of Jesus activity. They were, after all, not written for that purpose. They were intended as testimonies about Jesus. In this, the reality of faith and historical reality are interwoven. To a certain extent we can distinguish between these. The aspect of reality that can be verified, for example, by comparison with other reports or is due to an apparent contrast with the intention of the author can be called "historical." Accounts are normally more trustworthy when they are closer to what happened. The Gospels, too, can be dealt with in this way. It will mean that the aspect of faith figures implicitly.

Because *Mark* is the earliest Gospel, it must be the point of departure for our historical reconstruction. Besides Mark, as already mentioned, Matthew and Luke appear to have used a *sayings source*. To the extent that this is certain, we can view the relevant portions as an independent source alongside Mark. The oldest datable Christian writings, namely, the *letters of Paul*, are independent as well. The information about Jesus contained in these has historical priority.

In this manner we have *three independent early sources*. Starting from these, we must critically review the later reworkings in Matthew and Luke. Along with this we must also proceed to compare with the other sources, in the first place the ancient Jewish writings. In this Luke shows itself to be remarkably trustworthy. Because of the greater distance from Jesus' first disciples, the Gospel of John must be dealt with even more critically. It then becomes apparent that it nevertheless does contain all kinds of independent information.

The "Real" Jesus?

Can we in the manner suggested above finally get to know the real Jesus? Partially, yes; but partially, certainly not. To what extent do we ever really know someone, even someone with whom we live daily? In one way or another a person is always more than the totality of characteristics that can be listed. This is undoubtedly the case with Jesus. From the reports, we get the impression that he was a person with a strong effect upon others. With such an individual, it is difficult to figure out who he "really" is.

The reports in the Gospels relate how Jesus acted publicly. Here the reality of faith and historical reality are intertwined. My reconstruction is directed toward the historical aspect. Information from ancient Jewish sources provides additional help. I can summarize as follows: Jesus appeared with the prophetic message that God's kingdom was close at hand, taught that people should turn toward God, underscored his preaching with healings, and was condemned to death in Jerusalem by the chief priests. Such a historical reconstruction of his public ministry no doubt touches one side of the real Jesus.

The other aspect is the reality of faith. For the evangelists (the Gospel writers) and all of Jesus' other followers, this aspect was paramount. Here the significance for faith of his deeds is central. The evangelists testify to this especially by quotations from the Old Testament. That is, they recognized the special meaning of Jesus' behavior in what they read in the books of Moses and the prophets. Yet even this testimony of faith does not bring us further than his public ministry, the "exterior" of the real Jesus. Except for a small corner of the veil that is sometimes lifted for a moment, who he was in his own deepest self remains a secret for all time—even to faith.

3

The Jews in the Roman Empire

My aim is to consider the movement that emanated from Jesus and his first followers within its Jewish context. To that end we must read the New Testament and compare it closely with ancient Jewish sources. This in turn requires that we have a consistent picture of the world of Judaism within the Roman Empire. The sources portray the Judaism of that time as diversified. A good perspective on this can only be acquired from the two world empires that preceded Rome.

The Persian and Hellenistic Empires

Not everyone is aware that there are great differences between the religion of ancient Israel and the religion of Judaism. The name itself even expresses this: "Judaism" is spoken of only some time after the Babylonian exile.

Judaism as we know it must have acquired its form after the Babylonian exile. The exile ended around 550 B.C.E. with the victorious Persian campaign, which encompassed both Babylon and Jerusalem. Cyrus, the founder of the Persian Empire, allowed the Jews to return from Babylon to Jerusalem and to begin reconstructing their temple. This made Cyrus (pronounced in Hebrew "Koresh") highly popular among the Jews to the point that in the Bible he is even called God's "anointed" (Isaiah 45:1). After an interruption, the rebuilding was resumed a century later under the leadership of Ezra and Nehemiah, two Jewish officials of the Persian Empire. The biblical books bearing their names describe the operation. The political relationships are important: the reconstruction and reorganization of "Judaism" took place under the authority of the Persian king. (Ezra 1:1; Nehemiah 1:1; Isaiah 45:1)

The situation was different from the one before the exile, when there was a king in Jerusalem, and also for some time in the northern kingdom, which was then called "Israel." Though strategically dependent on powerful allies, these kings governed their own kingdoms. Opposite to them stood the prophets, who, as God's messengers, advocated righteousness and piety. The priests, in contrast, were more or less court functionaries. The religion of Israel had at that time a fairly limited horizon.

During the Persian era, the Jews had to learn to see themselves as a small ethnic minority in a world empire stretching from the Nile to the Indus River. For government business they had to use a foreign language, Aramaic. Parts of the book of Ezra and other portions of the Old Testament are written in this language. The Jews had their own "constitution" according to which they lived: the five books of Moses. This "law of the Jews" paralleled the constitutions of other ethnic minorities. A positive effect was that Judaism was a recognized religion within the Persian Empire. The constitutional recognition was maintained by later world empires.

On the other hand, in exile the Jews had experienced that God accompanied them everywhere. In this lies a paradox that has remained characteristic of Judaism. The dominion of Israel's God is worldwide and encompasses all peoples, while the people of Israel conduct their own, somewhat separate national existence. Judaism is a universal religion built on a particularistic basis.

Around 330 B.C.E., the Persian Empire was conquered in one brilliant campaign by a young general from Macedonia in northern Greece, Alexander, called "the Great." Enormous changes took place. The center of the world moved from the East to the West, and the lingua franca became Greek. What is commonly called the Hellenistic Empire emerged. "Hellenism," from "Hellas" (Greece), actually means "speaking Greek." Alexander died while still young, and the empire fell apart immediately. His generals founded kingdoms that in time varied in size. The most prominent two were the Graeco-Egyptian and the Graeco-Syrian kingdoms.

Much more than the Persians, the Macedonians aimed at exporting their favorite culture. That is why Greek statues and writings can be found in the far corners of the former Persian Empire. Everywhere educational institutions were founded and the Greek "classics" were taught. Locals ignorant of Greek did not count. Those who wanted to rise had to acquire a classical education. This ideal was taken over by the Romans, was revived during the Renaissance, and was rediscovered in the nineteenth century. It still exists, including its shortcomings, among which is a certain chauvinism.

On the other hand, there was also much that was not changed by the Macedonian conquest. Many administrative and financial structures of the Persians remained intact. The situation of the Jews and their law continued to be principally the same. Their recognized position within the framework of the Persian Empire was laid down in local treaties.

The Hellenistic world had two metropolises or "mother cities." Antioch, near the sea at the boundary of present-day Turkey and Syria, was the capital of the Graeco-Syrian kingdom. Alexandria, at the mouth of the Nile, was the capital of the Graeco-Egyptian kingdom. The latter truly was a world-trade center, where primarily grain and papyrus were exported. By means of the rich proceeds, Alexandria became the cultural capital of the world as well. It was known for some of the "seven wonders of the world," among which was the *Mousaion*, the "Muse temple" with the largest library in the world at that time.

In both cities many Jews dwelled; in Alexandria their numbers were between one-half million and one million. That is the background for the legend relating that the Graeco-Egyptian king had the law of Moses translated for his Mousaion library. It is indeed plausible that it was desirable to know what the "constitution" of the large Jewish community contained. Besides that, most of the Jews in these metropolises spoke Greek and even conducted their synagogue services in that language. The Greek translation will have been made partially for that purpose. The Greek translation, the *Septuagint*, comprises the Old Testament with somewhat more extensive contents than the Hebrew Bible. The additional material is retained by the Eastern Orthodox, Roman Catholic, and Lutheran churches. Calvinists and other Protestants keep themselves to the more limited compass of the Hebrew Bible. The Greek translation is of essential importance to the New Testament. When in the New Testament the Old Testament is referred to, the quotations are usually from the Septuagint.

At the beginning of the first century, there lived in Alexandria a philosopher and theologian named *Philo*. He creatively explained the Greek Bible text in a spiritual sense, thereby relating the most beautiful and profound elements of Greek thinking to Moses. He was a respected member of the Jewish community and was, for example, sent as a representative to Rome on a diplomatic mission. The links he made between theology and philosophy became highly influential among the church fathers, who preserved his works for this reason.

Opposition to the Hellenistic regime was eventually bound to arise. Leaders of local communities wanted to participate in the world empire but not be absorbed by it. The resistance took on various forms. A subtle form was the works of history in which Babylonian, Egyptian, and Jewish writers described the tradition of their own people—in Greek. When tensions rose too high, armed conflict could break out as well.

In 167 B.C.E., the Graeco-Syrian king Antiochus, nicknamed "Epiphanes" (manifestation [of God]), had an altar for the Greek god Zeus erected in the temple in Jerusalem. This religious interference deviated from the moderate politics of his predecessors. For the Jews it meant war. Priests who had excessively adapted to Hellenism were driven out of Jerusalem. The Jewish law was reinstated in honor, and in 164 B.C.E. the temple was rededicated. The Jewish festival of Hanukkah (Dedication) commemorates this event. The Jews founded their own state, which maintained itself for more than a century under the leadership of the priestly family with the nickname "Maccabee." Their history is described in the books by that name in the Septuagint. The book of Daniel also speaks of these occurrences, but in veiled language. (1 Maccabees 1:1; 2 Maccabees 1:1)

Thus two aspects of Jewish life in the Hellenistic world are exposed. Many Jews spoke, thought, and wrote in Greek and felt at ease with it. But when they felt threatened in their Jewish existence, they resisted—violently, if necessary.

The Roman Empire

Meanwhile, a new world power was asserting itself: Rome. Having conquered all of Italy, this metropolis proceeded to expand its dominance on all sides. Technique and organization made its armies almost invincible. Gradually Rome subdued the western portion of the Hellenistic kingdoms. The eastern part was taken over by a new Persian kingdom. In 31 B.C.E. the last Hellenistic kingdom, Egypt, fell into Roman hands, thus terminating the Hellenistic era in a strict sense. The conquering general, Octavian, was proclaimed emperor. Adorned with the name Augustus, "the illustrious," he laid the foundation for a lengthy dominion that he preferred to view as the *pax romana*, Roman world peace.

Again, much changed, but many things remained the same—language, for example. In the greater part of the Roman Empire, Greek continued to be used as a medium of communication. Even in the capital many immigrants spoke Greek. Thus it was that Paul wrote his letter to the church in Rome in Greek. For a long time the Roman church continued to use Greek in its liturgy, so that many contemporary churches would inherit the prayer, *Kyrie eleison*, "Lord, have mercy."

Another matter that did not change was the position of the Jews. The elevation of Judaism to a recognized religion was a ratification of the situation under the Hellenistic and Persian periods. Nonetheless, problems presented themselves. In Alexandria, for example, the Jews had to send a delegation to the emperor, among which was Philo. The emperor called for order but directed the Jews back to their place of being a recognized ethnic minority. Tensions did not always blow over. In 115 C.E. a revolt broke out among the Jews in another North African region, Cyrenaica (in contemporary Libya), and this spread to Alexandria as well. The non-Jewish population and the Roman government reacted fiercely. The result was the ruin of North African Jewry.

A new element under the Roman regime was taxes. These were much heavier than under the Hellenistic kingdoms and certainly than under the Persian Empire. Taxes were even more onerous because the Romans farmed out the collection of taxes to so-called publicans. These financial entrepreneurs did not lose sight of their own interests and were quite hated, as is apparent in the New Testament as well. Another odious element of Roman occupation was the forced labor to which the population was put for the construction of large projects such as theaters, aqueducts, and baths. Finally, the Roman system of slavery was unparalleled in antiquity. Roman industry and agriculture were based on large-scale slave trade. The worst was the metal mines, to which also political opponents were banned to face certain death.

The Jews in the Jewish Homeland

From 64 B.C.E. on, the Romans ruled in the Jewish homeland. The country had diverse names, and its status varied as well. The older, non-Jewish name was *Palaestina*. Jews usually called it then, as now, "the land of Israel." I use here a related term, "*the Jewish homeland*." The Romans incorporated it in 6 C.E. as the province of Judaea. Galilee was not as yet included in this but was governed by the relatives of Herod—first Antipas, then Agrippa.

The Jews in the province of Judaea were under a Roman governor who resided in the harbor town Caesarea. This town's ruins can still be seen halfway between Tel Aviv and Haifa. Important army contingents were stationed there as well. Of old the inner city was populated by non-Jews. The Jewish capital, Jerusalem, lay two days' march away. A Roman garrison was stationed there as well, which had its hands particularly full during the busy pilgrimage festivals. Pontius Pilate, who governed for ten years, was cruel and had little respect for the Jews. Other governors performed better.

Except for taxes and governors, many things remained the same. While world empires come and go, for ordinary people life goes on as usual. In the Jewish homeland various movements within society continued to appear. These had arisen during the Persian and Hellenistic eras and represented divergent concepts of Judaism. What they did have in common, however, was their dedication to the law of Moses, the foundation of Judaism established during the time of Ezra and Nehemiah. The differences lay in the interpretation of the law. Our information about these groups is partially direct and partially indirect.

Indirect information is available to us from the book of Daniel. It describes the Maccabean revolt against the Graeco-Syrian king in characteristically veiled, symbolic language. This way of expressing itself is characteristic of a particular, pious milieu. In this it resembles the apocalypse 1 Enoch. Both books speak in the same manner about the final judgment and mention a "Son of Man," a heavenly savior in human form. This manner of thinking, *apocalypticism*, has to do with the revelation of divine secrets concerning the future. Apocalyptic thinking is also found in the New Testament. Clearly related to these, for example, is the Revelation or Apocalypse of John. First Enoch is also cited verbatim in the Epistle of Jude. (pp. 2, 120)

The apocalyptic books of Daniel and Enoch played a significant role in Qumran as well. At this location on the Dead Sea, a large collection of scrolls was found in 1947. Together with the archeological situation, the scrolls render direct information about an important religious community that apparently was part of a broader movement, the *Essenes*. We know of the latter from the Graeco-Jewish writer Josephus, about whom more will be told later. He relates that the Essenes lived everywhere in the Jewish homeland. This could explain why their ideas were greatly influential even though the community itself was small. Their scrolls reveal an extremely closed conception of the world with a radical contrast between light and darkness. The sect members divided humanity, including the Jews, into "children of darkness" and "children of light." The latter expression occurs in the New Testament as well. Another characteristic of these Jews is that they attached great importance to ritual purity. In these and other points they were extremely strict in applying the Jewish law. (Ephesians 5:8; p. 3)

Given the fact that their influence was extensive, it is striking that the Essenes are mentioned neither in the New Testament nor in the Talmud. This makes it seem that they were hushed up—perhaps a reaction to the attitude of the Essenes themselves. In one of their scrolls they wrote that they had intentionally "separated themselves from the majority of the people." Some have suggested that John the Baptist and Jesus had been Essenes, but the silence about them in the New Testament makes this improbable.

Of direct significance to the New Testament and to the spiritual background of Jesus is the movement of the *Pharisees*. They comprised several schools of thought and enjoyed the most support from the general public. This will be pursued below.

There is one more prominent Jewish movement, the *Sadducees*. They were quite a small group of which we hear only from others; none of their own writings has been preserved. A conservative, partially Greek-speaking elite of high priestly families, they held sway in temple matters and were hated by the people because of their greediness. In contrast to most Jews, the Sadducees did not believe in angels, revelations, or the resurrection of the dead. They remained in power by the support of the Romans. In the New Testament they come to the fore as the sworn opponents of Jesus and his apostles. (p. 64)

Until the war with Rome, the leading trio consisted of Sadducees, Essenes, and Pharisees. That, at least, is what we understand from the most important historiographer of the war period, *Flavius Josephus*. Though himself a prominent priest, he was not a Sadducee but a Pharisee. He was a commander in the war but was soon captured. He then became a client of the Roman imperial family, Flavius, whose name he assumed and from whom he received an estate in Rome. His works of history are primarily written for non-Jewish readers, with the secondary objective of justifying his own behavior. As a rule, his detailed descriptions of the Jews in the Jewish homeland are trustworthy. (p. 92)

In 66 c.e. the first or "great" war of the Jews with Rome broke out. It was preceded by decades of rising tensions. In particular, an aversion to non-Jews had developed. Not all Jews, however, shared this sentiment. Many were against the war, which often rather resembled a civil war in which various groups strove for dominance. As a whole, the war must be seen in relation to the resistance against foreign domination, which the Jews had exhibited often. The successful revolt of the Maccabees in 167–164 b.c.e. has already been mentioned. A second war with Rome was to follow (132–135 c.e.). The great war ended in 70 c.e. with the destruction of the temple in Jerusalem. I will dwell on the calamitous effects later. (p. 14; chapter 7)

Somewhere in the midst of the three mentioned groups, there was a movement that deserves the most attention in this book. Information is not sufficient to delineate it clearly. It is the milieu from which Jesus and his disciples emerged. Josephus says but little about it. A few scattered reports appear in rabbinic literature. Most of the information derives from the New Testament itself. (See the schema on p. 139.)

The Pharisees and Rabbinic Literature

Because of their importance to Judaism itself and to the New Testament, the Pharisees need to be discussed separately. That is not possible without mentioning rabbinic literature as well, for there the thinking of the Pharisees is expressed most extensively and directly. Rabbinic literature includes the *Babylonian Talmud* and a series of commentaries on the Old Testament called the *Midrashim*. The most important portions were written down between the third and seventh centuries c.e.

For various reasons, Christian biblical interpreters do not normally use these writings in their studies. First, there are theological barriers related to the traditional antithesis between Christianity and Judaism. Since antiquity, the driving power of Judaism has lain in rabbinic tradition. Due to the traditional opposition, however, Christians have difficulties recognizing rabbinic literature as an instructive source of information about their own tradition of faith.

Historical hindrances also play a role. The earliest rabbinic texts were not written down until a century and a half after the New Testament. This fact must be treated in a level-headed manner. We can assume that rabbinic texts are the written deposit of a ramified oral tradition, in which portions are certainly much older than the date of writing. The process of oral transmission, however, implies variation as well, in spite of the care with which the rabbis, according to their own words, passed on the traditions of their teachers. Again, the comparison with other sources is essential. In particular the Dead Sea Scrolls and the writings of Josephus can help establish the antiquity of rabbinic traditions. Of special significance is the collection of rules of law (*halakah*). Strongly rooted in society, it forms an essential historical source whose transmission is relatively exact and trustworthy.

Finally, there is the difficulty of content. Roughly speaking, rabbinic literature represents but a part of the Pharisees of the first century, namely, the tradition of *Hillel*, a leader of the Pharisees who lived around the beginning of the common era. The composers of rabbinic literature idealize him as the founder of their tradition. The other Pharisaic movement was that of *Shammai*. Although at least as important in the first century as Hillel, Shammai and his school are cited much less. This situation is related to the outcome of the war with Rome and will be discussed below in chapter 7.

Many of Hillel's sayings have been transmitted. Sometimes they are short and difficult to understand, for example: "Do not separate yourself from the community." In this particular case, the discovery of the Dead Sea Scrolls comes to our aid. Hillel appears to be reacting to the Essene statement cited earlier: "We have separated ourselves from the majority of the people." Hillel emphasized that one must continue to communicate with other members of the community, even when disagreeing about religious insights or way of life—for the latter is at least as important in Judaism. (p. 17)

Further, the idea is ascribed to Hillel that the whole law of Moses can be summarized in one commandment, "Love your neighbor as yourself." This same concept is found in the Jesus tradition and in the letters of Paul. Again we see how crucial rabbinic literature is for comparison with the New Testament. (Leviticus 19:18; Mark 12:31; Romans 13:9; p. 48)

Hillel's colleague *Shammai* is portrayed as conservative and short-tempered. The contrast is schematic and reveals the significance later ascribed to these leaders. This reflects also on their manner of life. It is told that during the whole week Shammai was thinking about the coming Sabbath and was looking for lovely things to buy for it. Hillel thought in a different manner: every day must be dedicated to God. He thought about the Sabbath, too, but not as literally as Shammai did.

These are not isolated reports. Rabbinic literature relates that from the teachings of Shammai and Hillel two schools of learning issued. The disciples of Shammai were, according to tradition, stricter in the area of the Sabbath. They allowed fewer actions to be undertaken on the day of rest. The Dead Sea Scrolls shed unusual light upon this: they present a standpoint even stricter than that of the school of Shammai. Such differences in conceptions of the law are highly valuable to us. They enable us to position Jesus among his contemporaries. (p. 33)

Though in general the view of the school of Hillel was more flexible than that of Shammai, this was not true in all respects. In another prominent area, the rules of purity, the school of Hillel was more strict. The distinction is significant and demonstrates that we should not think of the Judaism of Jesus' day too schematically but must continually take exceptions into account.

There were also divergences in the attitude toward non-Jews. The school of Hillel was more open, that of Shammai more closed. The difference came strongly to the fore at the time of the war with Rome. The followers of Hillel were disinclined to war, but those of Shammai were eager to fight. At the beginning of the revolt, the Shammaites appear to have used violence to enforce a number of anti-Gentile regulations, by which they even victimized the Hillelites. This disparity in attitude is highly significant to the New Testament. (p. 92)

A separate question is how the *Jews in the diaspora* (that is, those outside the Jewish homeland) stood in relation to these Pharisaic schools. The sources give little information on this. In principle it could not have been much different from that in the Jewish homeland, though living as a Jewish minority would have brought other elements to the fore. When problems arose, one might more quickly feel threatened. Thus the defensive attitude toward Jesus' followers on the part of the young Paul, a Pharisee from Tarsus in Asia Minor, appears not to have been an exception. In all events, the tensions during the 50s and 60s were also clearly felt in the diaspora. (Acts 8:1)

4

Jesus and His Disciples

I have surveyed the development of the question of Jesus and the Jews throughout the ages. I have reflected on what in essence it is about, which documents belong in the dossier, and how these should be interpreted. I also have sketched an impression of the society and its movements from which the documents arose. I can now start hearing the witnesses. Beginning at the beginning: Who was Jesus, where did he come from, what did he come to do, how was he viewed by others—and by himself?

Apprenticeship with John the Baptist

The reports about Jesus' birth and youth provide little historical foothold. In quite different renderings, these can be found at the beginnings of Matthew and Luke. They can best be seen as legends intended to elucidate Jesus' special significance. This is an essential element in what we are investigating, but our approach demands that the historical aspect be treated first.

Elsewhere in the New Testament there are several scattered "personal data" that provide more foothold. According to a statement in Luke, Jesus was "about thirty years old when he began his work . . . the son (as was thought) of Joseph." There is no reason to doubt this information. In John, an excited disciple knows no better than that his new teacher is "Jesus, son of Joseph from Nazareth." This statement unreflectedly goes against later tradition and rings true. We hear more about his family in Mark. He preached in the synagogue of Nazareth, and his fellow citizens reacted with surprise and irritation: "Is this not the carpenter, the son of Mary and the brother of James and Joses and Jude and Simon, and are not his sisters here with us?" Also this report appears to be unfabricated. Later, in Matthew, the statement is altered to say that Jesus is the "carpenter's son." (Luke 3:23; John 1:45; Mark 6:3; Matthew 13:55)

Somewhat more problematic is the tradition that Jesus descended from King David. A letter of Paul, one of our oldest Christian documents, mentions this. The Davidic descent can no longer be verified, but it is not impossible. At that time, quite precise family trees were kept, especially in prominent families. In Jerusalem a stone coffin from Jesus' time has been found upon which is stated that the deceased was "of the house of David." (Romans 1:3)

Finally, there is no doubt at all that Jesus died on a Roman cross. This is affirmed everywhere, not only in the New Testament but also in ancient Christian creeds: he was "crucified under Pontius Pilate. . . ."

With this we have a profile of our main character. What do we know about his *activity*? We must begin where Mark, the oldest Gospel, does: at his baptism by John. Not much is known about the figure of John the Baptist, but there is no doubt about his existence. Josephus also reports his activities and his popularity: John summoned people to turn to God sincerely and to let themselves be baptized by him; many took him to be a righteous prophet. This concurs with the report in Mark, in which the Baptist is depicted as being at the center of a movement in which Jews came to confess their sins and to submit to his "baptism of repentance for the forgiveness of sins." (Mark 1:4)

Our sources tell little more about the Baptist's movement, but we can indirectly gather some insights into it. In Mark, the Baptist is introduced with the words of the prophet Isaiah: "A voice cries out, 'In the wilderness prepare the way of the Lord.'" In the Dead Sea Scrolls, the same text was applied to the Essene community. They, too, issued a call to repentance and to a reform of Judaism. Immersion as a sign of purity of spirit and body played a central role in this. There are also other prophetic texts associated both with John and Jesus and also with the Essene community. This does not necessarily mean that John belonged to that community. We have noted that the New Testament ignores the Essenes. The Baptist as we know him must have belonged to a reform movement that at least partially followed the same traditions as the Essenes but that "did not separate itself from the community." (Isaiah 40:3; p. 17)

Jesus joined this movement. As though it were a most natural occurrence, Mark relates that Jesus submitted to John's baptism of "repentance for the forgiveness of sins." Which sins did Jesus then have? The account in Mark does not explain. What counts is that Jesus put repentance and forgiveness foremost for himself as well. Later Gospel writers had difficulty conceiving of how this could be: should not John rather have been baptized by Jesus? The reaction is interesting, because it assumes that Jesus performed baptisms as well. This is indeed confirmed by an exceptional report in the Gospel of John. (Mark 1:9; Matthew 3:14; John 3:22)

It thus seems that Jesus was a disciple of the Baptist for some time. If this is correct, it is our only information about Jesus' teachers. His preaching has so much in common with the Pharisees that he also must have studied in their circles. But, except for the legend about the twelve-year-old Jesus in the temple, we have no reports of this. (Luke 2:42)

According to the accounts, the relationship between John and Jesus was actually the reverse: John said of himself that he was too insignificant to "untie the thong of [Jesus'] sandals," a service that a disciple is supposed to do for his teachers. Although the evangelist thereby underscores Jesus' importance, the possibility is not excluded that John saw Jesus as an exceptional disciple. However that may be, several statements of Jesus have been handed down that stress differences with John. John was the greatest among the prophets, but "the least in the kingdom of God." In comparison to the austere desert prophet, Jesus called himself the "bridegroom," the one who brought "new wine." (Mark 1:7; Luke 7:28, 36; Mark 2:18)

In these statements, tradition ascribes to Jesus an unusual awareness of a calling. Other reports bring this out as well. According to Mark, Jesus had a vision immediately after he was baptized: "He saw the heavens torn apart and the Spirit descending like a dove on him. And a voice came from heaven, 'You are my Son, the Beloved; with you I am well pleased.'" Subsequently he was tested in the desert by the devil. The impression is given that Jesus had a bent for mysticism and that at his baptism he knew himself to be called to a special task. A corner of the impenetrable veil that shrouds his personality is lifted. (Mark 1:10)

Jesus' Gospel

The opening section of Mark is remarkable in two respects. It is quite concise, but in that conciseness it supplies remarkable details. The announcement that immediately follows Jesus' baptism is brief: John the Baptist was imprisoned. Only later are the reasons for this given, as the introduction to the story of the Baptist's execution. In the account of Jesus' first public appearance, this does not yet play a role. (Mark 6:14)

Exceptional details are also provided in this account of Jesus' first public appearance: "After John was arrested, Jesus came to Galilee, proclaiming the good news of God, and saying, 'The time is fulfilled, and the kingdom of God has come near; repent, and believe in the good news.'" (Mark 1:14)

Some explanation is required. The concept *kingdom of God* means simply that God is king; in other words, it refers to the dominion of God. The background for this lies in the book of Daniel, which has been mentioned already. The notion has to do with God's coming world dominion in which his faithful ones will receive justice and unjust rulers will be punished. According to Jesus, this was just around the corner. And that is *good news* or, in the Greek, *evangel*. The word comes from yet another biblical text from Isaiah. There the prophet states that he was sent by God "to bring good news to the oppressed." These words from Isaiah were apparently crucial to Jesus. (Daniel 7:27; Isaiah 61:1)

The words from Isaiah also recur in the so-called *Beatitudes*. The first one says: "Blessed are you who are poor, for yours is the kingdom of God." The poor are the same as those in the prophecy of Isaiah; to them good news is promised. According to Luke, Jesus' first sermon in the synagogue in Nazareth also had these words as its text. In yet another passage, Jesus summarized his ministry with a string of these and related prophetic words: "The blind receive their sight, the lame walk, . . . the dead are raised, the poor have good news brought to them." Jesus' message was saturated with the study of the prophets and other biblical writings. (Luke 4:18; 6:20; 7:22; Matthew 5:3; 11:5)

According to Mark, Jesus, in line with John and the biblical prophets, brought "*the gospel of God.*" This, too, is an exceptional expression. We are accustomed to hear the word "gospel" as a message *about* Jesus. Here it is his *own* message, the good news that he himself was bringing about God's dominion. This is the core of his ministry.

This good news, this gospel, involves a summons to repentance, to turn around. People must turn their lives toward God and change in accordance with God's dominion. In this Jesus apparently linked up with his teacher. It was not without reason that just before his public ministry he wanted to undergo the baptism of repentance. God's dominion was at hand, but people must take the first step. Seen in this way, baptism is an act of recognizing God's dominion and an expression of the desire to prepare the way. We have seen that apparently Jesus also baptized others. Christian baptism evidently originated with Jesus himself, who, in turn, adopted it from his teacher, John.

According to the account in Mark, it is a "baptism of repentance for the forgiveness of sins"—words that have an important place in the teachings of Jesus as well. The best-known text ascribed to him is the prayer he taught his disciples, the "Lord's Prayer." In it the prayers for the coming of the kingdom of God and for forgiveness of sins stand side by side. These were common themes in Jewish prayers of that time. Jesus gave them a central place in his preaching, and he also called others to follow this path. The first step along that road is baptism—as a recognition of God's dominion, as a request for forgiveness of sins, and as a resolution to do his will. (Luke 11:2; Matthew 6:9)

This sounds serious, and it is. At the same time, however, Jesus' message is cheerful and liberating. He said, "Whoever does not receive the kingdom of God *as a little child* will never enter it." And, "Look at the birds of the air; they neither sow nor nor reap nor gather into barns, and yet your heavenly Father feeds them. Are you not of more value than they? . . . Strive first for the kingdom of God. . . ." A woman tearfully anointed his feet with a costly ointment. "She is a sinner," a Pharisee observed. Jesus recognized her true longing and said: "Her sins, which were many, have been forgiven; *hence she has shown great love.*" It is a message loaded with merciful humor. This is how people should forgive one another as well: "Be children of your Father in heaven; for he makes his sun shine on the evil *and* on the good, and sends rain on the righteous *and* on the unrighteous." (Mark 10:15; Matthew 6:26; Luke 7:39; Matthew 5:45)

Jesus not only proclaimed this gospel himself but, according to a report in the first three Gospels, also sent out his disciples to do the same. They were to go out and proclaim the message of their master. This report contains peculiar details that point to its origin in a specific tradition: they were not to take along any luggage, bread, money, or extra clothes. Dependent on the hospitality of their audience, they were to stay with those who listened to them and to turn away from those who did not. Thus their whole existence was focused on preaching Jesus' good news. It is striking that this tradition is confirmed by someone who had not himself witnessed Jesus' teaching, namely, Paul. In a passage on the sustenance of the apostles, he wrote, "The Lord commanded that those who proclaim the gospel should get their living by the gospel.""The Lord" here means Jesus. (Mark 6:8; Matthew 10:5; Luke 9:1; 10:1; 1 Corinthians 9:14)

Jesus' disciples are called *apostles* in this context. The designation derives from Jewish usage and literally means "emissaries." An emissary acts on behalf of the one who give the commission, and the response that his mission receives reflects directly on the one who sent him. Such relationships are codified both in rabbinic literature and in a saying attributed to Jesus: "Whoever listens to you listens to me, and whoever rejects you rejects me, and whoever rejects me rejects the one who sent me." The preaching of the "apostles" is thus an extension of Jesus' own preaching. (Luke 10:16)

An important general conclusion can be drawn. The gospel with which Jesus came and with which he dispatched his disciples was a reform movement *within Judaism*. A tradition in Matthew, according to which Jesus saw himself and his disciples as having been sent "to the lost sheep of the house of Israel," confirms this. (Matthew 10:6; 15:24)

Jesus and the Jewish Law

Since the time of Ezra and Nehemiah, the law was reckoned as the basis of living for all Jews. But opinions diverged concerning its interpretation.

The next question therefore is: What position did Jesus' reform movement take toward the law?

Previous generations of theologians were convinced that Jesus had *abolished* the Jewish law. There are now only a few who would still assert this. It is becoming more and more of a consensus that Jesus was a Jew who kept the law in his own manner. The disputed question is the *interpretation* he gave to it. In his time, this question was posed precisely so among the Jews themselves. Several times, it was the *Pharisees* who put this question to Jesus. This speaks volumes. Josephus relates that the Pharisees were generally considered to be the most expert interpreters of the law and in this enjoyed the trust of the people. According to rabbinic literature, this was their striving and their ambition. (p. 95)

In a passage that occurs only in Matthew, Jesus summarized his position on the law: "Do not think that I have come to abolish the law or the prophets; I have come not to abolish but to fulfill." In the verses that follow, the significance of the statement is explained. Not one of "the least of these commandments" can be annulled, and he who does so is "least" in the kingdom of God. Examples are added to make this concrete, examples that give *Jesus' interpretation of the law.* A familiar "great" commandment is, "You shall not kill." According to Jesus, this also included an implicit commandment: you may not call your neighbor names or wish him dead. In the same manner, for Jesus the commandment "You shall not commit adultery" included the implicit prohibition of looking lustfully at your neighbor's wife. (Matthew 5:17)

Expressions like "annulling the law" and "the least commandment" bring to mind Pharisaic terms known from rabbinic literature. There we also find correspondences in content with the "small commandments" of Jesus. These rabbinic elements contradict the later development of the Gospel of Matthew and thus suggest for Matthew's assertions on this matter a certain trustworthiness. Theologians now and in the past have had difficulty imagining that Jesus had such Pharisaic opinions, but Jesus proclaimed ideas concerning the law that went even much further. A striking example has to do with divorce.

Divorce was a topic of the law hotly debated among the Jews of that time. Three positions are distinguishable. The Pharisees thought divorce to be possible in principle, but differed concerning the conditions. The

Hillelites were the most permissive. They read in the law of Moses that a marriage could be dissolved by a husband if he found "something objectionable" in his wife, after which both of the ex-partners could remarry. This interpretation set the tone in rabbinic literature and still holds in Judaism. The followers of Shammai, however, read the law to mean that divorce is possible only in the case of adultery or some other sexual misbehavior. The strictest position was to be found among the Essenes. The Dead Sea Scrolls insist on the interpretation that one may not remarry as long as the partner is still alive. This amounts to complete prohibition of divorce. (Deuteronomy 24:1)

These facts help in reconstructing the background of the Pharisees' questions concerning Jesus' interpretation of the law. The account in Mark seems the most trustworthy. The Pharisees asked: "Is it lawful for a man to divorce his wife?" Jesus answered with the question about what they read in the law; they responded by referring to the divorce regulation of "Moses" (as in Deuteronomy 24:1). Jesus rejected this as a concession to human weakness and pointed instead to the creation story. There Jesus read the original divine intention: one man and one woman, created for each other and therefore inseparable until death. Note, first, that it is impossible to state that Jesus here abolished the law. Second, it appears that on this important point Jesus shared the Essene interpretation. This is exceptional. There are other topics where he certainly thought in a non-Essene manner, for example, concerning the Sabbath (see below). The Pharisees apparently had reason to question where Jesus stood on the matter of divorce. (Mark 10:2; Genesis 1:26; 2:24)

Judging from early Christian sources, most of the followers of Jesus adopted Jesus' rejection of divorce. On this point of the law they were stricter than the Pharisees! This is particularly remarkable in the case of Paul. As a Pharisee he must have followed either the viewpoint of Shammai or that of Hillel. He abandoned this, however, for Jesus' stricter interpretation of the law. Paul applied this even to the legal situation of non-Jews, where the woman was allowed to take the initiative in divorce. We find the same in Mark. This strict Jewish rule was thus also valid for non-Jews. Not all Christians, however, followed Jesus in this. According to Matthew, divorce is allowed in the case of adultery or sexual misbehavior. This accords with the Pharisaic school of Shammai. It is a significant moderation of Jesus' radical standpoint. (1 Corinthians 7:10; Mark 10:12; Matthew 5:31; 19:9)

The keeping of the *Sabbath* was also a topic on which the Jews differed. A comparable spectrum of viewpoints can be observed: the Essenes very strict, the school of Shammai less so, and the school of Hillel the most permissive. The Pharisees did agree on the principle that the care of human life surpassed the Sabbath. This had been decided during the Maccabean wars, after a number of Jews chose to let themselves be killed rather than to violate the Sabbath. Among the arguments brought forward by the rabbis is the proverbial calf in a well. If a calf has fallen in a well on the Sabbath, one may take care that it remains alive. If a person is involved, one may even break down the well! All actions are allowed for the preservation of human life. Biblical arguments were found to support this. To the expression, The "Sabbath is holy *for you*," the rabbis linked the saying, "*For you* is the Sabbath ordained, not you for the Sabbath." (Exodus 31:14; p. 18)

It is thus not surprising that the Pharisees came to Jesus with questions about this issue as well. They saw his disciples plucking kernels from ears of grain and eating them, and they asked: "Why are they doing what is not lawful on the sabbath?" Jesus thought that it was permitted. His answer contains a sentence that strongly resembles the rabbinic saying mentioned: "The sabbath was made for humankind, and not humankind for the sabbath." Further, there are various reports about healings Jesus performed on the Sabbath. The Pharisees watched closely what he did. He noticed that and posed a question, "Is it lawful to cure on the Sabbath?" He then referred to the sheep falling into a pit. This shows that Jesus entered into genuine discussion with the Pharisees. He could support his actions by their own arguments. (Mark 2:23; Matthew 12:11)

What was the Pharisees' reaction to Jesus' words about the Sabbath? Here the Gospels differ. In most of the Gospels we read that the Pharisees wanted to kill Jesus because of his behavior on the Sabbath. This reaction is not consistent with any of the Jewish sources of that time. Luke, however, states several times that the Pharisees did not know what to do with him. They were not at ease with what he did, but they could not catch him in a real violation. This sounds probable. Apparently Jesus healed on the Sabbath in a manner that disturbed the Pharisees, but they could not condemn him (I will return to this later). (Luke 6:11; 14:6; pp. 105, 109)

From these examples it is apparent that Jesus' interpretation of the law found its place between that of the Essenes and the Pharisees. At times he appeared to agree with the one, at times with the other. Jesus would not have been the only one to have occupied such a position. We might think of the movement to which his teacher, John the Baptist, belonged, but this remains conjecture. Our information about the Judaism of that time is too scanty.

The Master and His Disciples

One aspect of how Jesus acted has direct links to rabbinic literature, namely, his relation to his disciples. This was also a major theme for the rabbis. One of the few things the Talmud tells about Jesus is that he had five disciples. According to some, this was the ideal number. At the beginning of the Gospel of John, Jesus is indeed said to have *five* disciples. It could be that this is an original account. Elsewhere in the Gospels, the *twelve* apostles are central. Twelve represents a different theme and has to do with the dispatching of the disciples as emissaries. Twelve is the number of the tribes of ancient Israel who, according to tradition, will be reinstated in the kingdom of God, in the future redemption. In contrast, the five have to do only with the relation between a teacher and his disciples. (John 1:37; Mark 3:14; 6:7; Matthew 19:28)

The Talmud relates how teachers discussed with their disciples at length all types of questions while they were on the road, while they rested during the heat of the day, or in other everyday situations. A teacher and his disciples traveled together, ate together, celebrated the Sabbath and the feast days together, and lived together. Such a personal bond between teacher and pupil was sometimes also found in Greek schools of philosophy. It was typical that the teachings of the master were learned by heart.

All these aspects can be found in the relationship of Jesus and his disciples. On the road questions were asked and answered, such as who was the most important among the disciples. They ate together in a house where they were invited or in the open field. As at Jewish meals, the teacher pronounced a blessing at the breaking of the bread. Jesus' disciples even had their money communally; Judas kept the purse. Luke summarizes it as follows: Jesus "went on through cities and villages, proclaiming and bringing the good news of the kingdom of God. The twelve were with him, as well as some women . . . who provided for them out of their resources." (Mark 10:32; 6:41; John 12:6; Luke 8:1)

Among these rich women, so we are told in Luke, was Martha. She received Jesus and his company into her house and cared diligently for them. She was irritated with her younger sister, Mary, who just sat and listened to Jesus. But Jesus said that Mary, as his disciple, "has chosen the better part, which will not be taken away from her." Although this story occurs only in Luke, it confirms a characteristic of Jesus found also in the other Gospels. Like the rest of the ancient world, Judaism was a man's society, even though there were internal differences. For the Essenes, a woman hardly counted. Like certain Pharisees, however, Jesus thought that women should be allowed to study. This remained, however, an exception, and in this matter the later church was not an improvement. (Luke 10:38)

It might appear that Martha in her care for material matters had chosen "the wrong portion," and this conclusion is not entirely wrong. Jesus was critical of possessions—or as the Pharisees called it, of "mammon." To a rich man who wanted to follow him, Jesus said that he must sell his possessions and give to the poor. Jesus did not say this to everybody, but he intended it fully seriously. This radical attitude differed from that of the Pharisees. Rabbinic literature tells of an Arab prince, also mentioned by Josephus, who wanted to become Jewish. He gave away his possessions to acquire "a treasure in heaven" but was reprimanded by the Pharisees. They had a rule that a maximum of one-fifth of one's possessions could be given away; otherwise there would be chaos in society. Jesus was more conscious of the dangers of riches. His disciples adopted this from him: it is said that the first Christians in Jerusalem shared their possessions. (Matthew 19:21; Acts 4:32)

Jesus not only stayed in the houses of those who had joined themselves to him but went also to *tax collectors*, that hated group that was considered to be extortioners and collaborators. Jesus' action caused tensions with the Pharisees. Just as with the "woman of ill repute," Jesus saw these publicans in the light of God's coming kingdom and therefore in the light of the possibility of conversion. It is no coincidence that there are two stories of tax collectors who repented. Conversely, according to Luke, Jesus let himself be invited by Pharisees as well. On such occasions there were sharp confrontations, but the relationship was not broken off. (Mark 2:14; Luke 7:36; 11:37; 14:1; 19:8; p. 26)

While on the road or when resting, Jesus taught continuously. Just as with the rabbis, the disciples must have learned the more important lessons and rules by heart. For Western readers this may seem unlikely, but there still are cultures where whole collections of stories or laws are transmitted orally. The Quran, too, is recited by heart. The church fathers report that the transmission of Jesus' words continued to be done orally for a long time. This is understandable in the culture in which Jesus lived.

From rabbinic literature it is apparent that oral transmission was preferred by the Pharisees as well. Oral transmission is characterized by succinctness and the use of fixed formulations to aid the memory. This makes it impossible to determine exactly what the speaker himself had said. When after some time the tradition is committed to writing, further changes occur. The recorder must choose between various traditions and also organize and structure the material to some extent. (p. 4)

The written texts still preserve some characteristics of oral tradition, for example, the use of numbers in the sayings of the rabbis: "There are four types of disciples: the funnel, which lets everything flow through, the sponge, which absorbs everything, the wine strainer, which lets the good pass through but retains the bad, and the winnow, which lets the chaff blow away and retains the good." Similarly, Jesus told the parable of four kinds of earth: the path where the seed is picked away, the rocky ground where it cannot take root, the field full of weeds where the plant has to make room to expand, and the good earth where it can take root and bear much fruit. (Mark 4:3)

Such comparisons with rabbinic literature can sometimes suggest how Jesus must have formulated his teachings, or in any event how his disciples remembered them. This is not equally true everywhere. The transmitted teachings of Jesus were processed in the Gospels by each evangelist in his own way. In the preceding oral transmission, all kinds of elements could have been changed. As mentioned above, the Gospel of John diverges widely in language and style. Probably the first three Gospels reflect the wording of Jesus the most purely.

"Who Do People Say that I Am?"

Jesus' ministry evoked discussion. The question of his person belongs to the core of his mission and influence, both during his lifetime and afterwards. In later chapters I pursue the answers given by others. Here it is fitting to see how he himself thought about it.

Jesus' concept of himself is a fundamental aspect of his historical person. He was not like other teachers of the law, as we hear from Mark: "He taught them as one having authority." And he was apparently aware of this. Everything we hear about him indicates an exceptional personality who went his own way. We observe this in his relationship to his teacher, John. In this self-awareness, Jesus was not literally unique. In certain Dead Sea Scrolls a remarkable personality expresses himself. Rabbinic literature and Josephus as well tell of somewhat comparable pious individuals. The Baptist himself could be counted among these. (Mark 1:22; p. 28)

Our best starting point is a report in Matthew and Luke that might come from the "sayings source." From prison John the Baptist sent two of his disciples to Jesus with the question: "Are you the one who is to come, or are we to wait for another?" Part of Jesus' answer has been cited already: "Go and tell John what you have seen and heard: the blind receive their sight, the lame walk, the lepers are cleansed, the deaf hear, the dead are raised, and the poor have good news brought to them." "The one who is to come" must be a designation for the servant of God or the Messiah who would usher in redemption. Jesus thus answered John's question of whether he was the coming one affirmatively. He did this by pointing to the signs of deliverance that took place through him. In doing so, he employed phrases derived from the biblical prophets, especially from Isaiah. (Luke 7:18; Matthew 11:2)

A song of praise found in Qumran provides the account with a historical perspective. Composed of biblical expressions strung together, especially from the prophets, the Qumran hymn describes how God and the Messiah "liberate prisoners, restore sight to the blind, . . . cause the dead to revive, and proclaim good news to the meek." The closing words in particular make clear that we are dealing with a cognate tradition. It does not appear to be specific to the Qumran community, but it is related to their future expectations. This text can be taken as supporting the historical probability of such a conversation between Jesus and John.

In another account, this time from Mark, Jesus posed his disciples the fundamental question: "Who do people say that I am?" The report occupies a pivotal position in this Gospel. Mark is composed of two main parts: the first deals with Jesus' work in Galilee, while the second is dominated by the crucifixion in Jerusalem. The division between the two is clearly marked by this question. Immediately thereafter, Jesus announced for the first time that he "must be killed." Then comes the story of his "transfiguration" in the presence of three disciples on top of the mountain; Jesus was transfigured in heavenly glory. These dramatic happenings bring out the intention of the evangelist, but they do not as yet bring Jesus' own motives into view. (Mark 8:27)

Given the question of John the Baptist, such a conversation about Jesus' significance is not improbable. The answers to the question of public opinion about Jesus that the disciples pass on are certainly conceivable: Some said "John the Baptist; and others, Elijah; and still others, one of the prophets." What is described here also appears in various forms in the texts of Josephus and those from Qumran. The Jews of that day entertained a series of vivid expectations concerning the coming redemption, in which Elijah played an important role—as did "the prophet," John the Baptist, who, according to this report, had already been executed. (Apparently, there was speculation about the possibility of the Baptist's resurrection; some thought that Jesus was John resurrected.) (Mark 8:28)

Jesus was completely at home with these expectations and related them to himself as well. We find this in a number of short sayings attributed to him. Separately, they provide little to hold onto historically, but, taken together, they exhibit a characteristic pattern: "I have come to call not the righteous but sinners"; "Do not think that I have come to abolish the law or the prophets; I have come not to abolish but to fulfill"; "Do not think that I have come to bring peace to the earth; I have not come to bring peace, but a sword." The last two sayings were possibly adapted during transmission. These sayings express an awareness of someone who has "come" with an unusual task in history. We can also hear an echo of the answer to John the Baptist: Jesus viewed himself as "the one who is to come." He acted with an unusual consciousness of calling. (Mark 2:17; Matthew 5:17; 10:34)

The conversation in Mark about "Who do people say that I am?" has an interesting conclusion: "He asked them, 'But who do you say that I am?'

Peter answered him, 'You are the Messiah.' And he sternly ordered them not to tell anyone about him." The word "Messiah" or "Anointed" (*mashiah* in Aramaic, *christos* in Greek) is not used often by Mark. Nonetheless, Peter's confession accords with the evangelist's intention. Why then does he have Jesus respond with so much reserve? Does he want to fully disclose the implications of this confession only at the end? Or are we faced here with Jesus' own reserve toward the title Messiah? These questions are difficult to unravel. But the result is the same: according to Mark's story, the title Messiah (Christ) does not fit well with Jesus' behavior. Later, as we know, this came to be the title most frequently applied to him. (Mark 8:29)

Jesus' own consciousness of a calling comes more to the fore in two other expressions, *Son of Man* and *Son of God*. Earlier scholars had difficulty accepting the idea that Jesus could have used such expressions of himself. The discoveries at Qumran have changed this. I mentioned above the use of the term "Son of Man" in the books of Daniel and Enoch, which were valued at Qumran. In these book the expression "Son of Man" is a Semitic manner of referring to a heavenly figure "in human form." He would appear when God pronounces final judgment in the presence of "tens of thousands of angels." The exact phrase "Son of God" (in the singular) does not occur in the Old Testament, but it does appear in another text from Qumran, in which the royal redeemer is called the "son of God" and "son of the Most High." (p. 28)

Jesus designated himself as the Son of Man whenever he spoke of the reason for his "coming" and of his destiny. Sometimes this involved other matters than those treated in Daniel and Enoch. Jesus is recorded as saying not only that "the Son of Man" would come on the clouds with his angel but also that "the Son of Man came not to be served but to serve, and to give his life a ransom for many." With respect to these texts, it is difficult to discern exactly what he actually said. The concept that the heavenly savior must *suffer and die* had not been encountered in ancient Jewish texts, until it was recently found in certain Qumran hymns. It is therefore no longer necessary to ascribe the concept to the later church. It appears that Jesus himself adopted and developed this thought. (Mark 13:26; 10:45; Daniel 7:13)

The most enigmatic is the expression Son (of God). In this we come closest to the "secret" of the historical Jesus. The expression never comes directly from his own mouth. Twice a heavenly voice said to him, "You are my Son, the Beloved." Once was at his baptism; I read the account in Mark as a mystical calling before the onset of his public ministry. The other time was at his transfiguration on the mountain. This, too, was a mystical experience apparently intended as a confirmation of his calling before the journey to Jerusalem. It was always someone else who called him Son of God, for example, the evil spirits and the centurion at the cross. According to Mark's account, Jesus confirmed the explicit question of the high priest as to whether he was the Son of God, but, according to the other Gospels, he answered only indirectly. (Mark 1:11; 3:11; 5:7; 9:7; 14:61; 15:39)

The biblical echoes in this expression are significant. One echo is that of Isaac, Abraham's "beloved son," who, according to the divine command, had to be "offered" by his father. Only when God saw that the father did not spare his son was a substitute sacrifice accepted. Another biblical echo is that of the songs of the servant of God in Isaiah who suffers for others. As with the expression Son of Man, these are biblical terms used to express Jesus' special calling. Dying for others is a part of this. In all events, his earliest disciples understood it in this manner. (Genesis 22:2; Isaiah 42:1; 53:4)

One utterance of Jesus himself related to this is his characteristic form of address in prayer. A number of prayers scattered throughout the four Gospels use the simple opening "Father." Jesus expressed in this manner his sense of having a special relationship to God. The prayer just previous to his arrest, according to Mark, is striking: "Abba, Father, for you all things are possible; remove this cup from me; yet, not what I want, but what you want." The expression of mortal agony lends this account an authentic ring. The evangelist gives the form of address in Aramaic with a Greek translation for his readers. Paul reports that the same Aramaic form of address was used in his churches, thus pointing to an imitation of the tradition of Jesus. The phenomenon was perhaps not unique. In rabbinic literature a manner of address as of a "son" to his "Father" is ascribed to certain pious individuals. (Matthew 11:25; Mark 14:36; Luke 11:2; John 12:27; Romans 8:15)

Concern for the Holiness of the Temple

Jesus' public ministry led up to an event whose crucial importance is often misunderstood. It provides an unexpected insight into the manner in which he saw himself and his task. Around Passover he traveled with his disciples to Jerusalem. Upon his arrival, according to Mark, he went to the temple mount and "looked around at everything." He then lodged in a village close by. The next day he went again to the temple. This time he began to expel violently all those selling animals for sacrifice and the moneychangers who had their business there. He explained his action by means of biblical phrases that the temple was not to be a "den of robbers" but a "house of prayer." (Mark 11:11)

The so-called cleansing of the temple was not a sudden whim. Jesus had closely observed the situation the day before. Many more indications scattered throughout various sources confirm this impression and provide a coherent picture. What Jesus did in the temple appears to have been premeditated and deliberate.

First, the temple occupies a special place in many of Jesus' sayings. What recurs is the desire for purity of devotion in the place where God's merciful presence is especially evident. Thus it is that Jesus told an exemplary story about a Pharisee and a tax collector who both came to the temple. The Pharisee was pleased with himself and thanked God that he was not like that bad tax collector. "But the tax collector, standing far off, would not even look up to heaven, but was beating his breast [out of remorse] and saying, 'God be merciful to me, a sinner.'" Jesus went on to say, "I tell you, this man went down to his home justified rather than the other." In another saying, Jesus advised, "When you are offering your gift at the altar, if you remember that your brother or sister has something against you, leave your gift there before the altar and go; first be reconciled to your brother or sister, and then come and offer your gift." Jesus also appeared completely serious in stating that swearing by the temple does not show true respect: "Whoever swears by the sanctuary, swears by it and by the one who dwells in it." (Luke 18:13; Matthew 5:23; 23:21)

Second, there are many stories that show that Jesus and his family were devoted to the temple. Luke repeats several times that Joseph and Mary went with their newborn child to the temple and fulfilled "everything required by the law of the Lord." "Every year his parents went to Jerusalem for the festival of the Passover." On one such occasion, Jesus remained behind in the temple to talk with the teachers, while his parents traveled a whole day on the return journey. These are legends, of course, but they could contain truth. In other reports, it is told that Jesus' brother James, the leader of the first church, continually went to the temple to pray. The same is said of the earliest church itself. Finally, according to the Gospel of John, during his public ministry Jesus went at least four times to Jerusalem for a festival. (Luke 2:39; Acts 2:46; John 2:13; 5:1; 7:10; 12:1)

Third, there are several statements in which Jesus expressed criticism of the officials of the temple administration. At the temple mount he warned against the scribes who love to walk about in distinguished mantles and to sit in prominent places in the synagogues. They recite long prayers while they "devour widows' houses." In contrast, he praised a poor widow whom he saw cast two coins into the collection box, "she . . . has put in all she had to live on." He accused the lawyers connected to the temple administration of hypocrisy: "You build the tombs of the prophets whom your ancestors killed . . . so that this generation may be charged with the blood of all the prophets shed since the foundation of the world, from the blood of Abel to the blood of Zechariah, who perished between the altar and the sanctuary." Jesus here used the widespread motif of the murder of prophets. According to legend, both Isaiah and Jeremiah were martyred as well. (Luke 20:45; 21:2; 11:47)

Fourth, a highly personal motivation of Jesus appears to play a role: "'Jerusalem, Jerusalem, the city that kills the prophets and stones those who are sent to it! How often have I desired to gather your children together as a hen gathers her brood under her wings, and you were not willing! See, your house is left to you. . . .'" (I return shortly to this enigmatic prediction.) In another report we read, "As he came near and saw the city, he wept over it, saying, 'If you, even you, had only recognized on this day the things that make for peace! But now they are hidden from your eyes.'" (Luke 13:34; Matthew 23:37; Luke 19:41)

That the city and the temple moved him comes out in a remarkable report in Luke: "At that very hour some Pharisees came and said to him, 'Get away from here, for Herod [Antipas] wants to kill you.' He said to them, 'Go and tell that fox for me, "Listen, I am casting out demons and performing cures today and tomorrow, . . . and the next day I must be on my way, because it is impossible for a prophet to be killed outside of Jerusalem."'" The unusual fact that Pharisees were concerned for his life makes an authentic impression. Particularly striking is that Jesus viewed himself as a prophet who must die in Jerusalem. Luke states this at an important turning point in his narrative, using these words: Jesus "set his face to go to Jerusalem." Such an expression is used often in Ezekiel, where this prophet receives the assignment to prophesy, among other things "against Jerusalem." (Luke 13:31; 9:51; Ezekiel 21:2)

Fifth, as noted above, statements are transmitted in which Jesus foretold his own death in Jerusalem. In the first three Gospels, an additional three of these occur. In the case of each of these "passion predictions," his disciples did not grasp the significance. Jesus says that he would be "rejected by the elders, the chief priests, and the scribes, and be killed, and after three days rise again." Later readers hear echoes of the familiar words of the creed. Nonetheless, the report that the disciples did not understand what Jesus meant is striking. It is as though they subsequently became aware that Jesus had been intending something that he had not made clear to them. (Mark 8:31; 9:31; 10:32)

Sixth, yet another prediction is ascribed to Jesus—the destruction of the temple. The account in Luke of Jesus' lament over the city continues as follows: "The days will come upon you, when your enemies will set up ramparts around you . . . and they will not leave within you one stone upon another." Apart from Luke another form of the saying occurs both in Mark and Matthew: "As he came out of the temple, one of the disciples said to him, 'Look, Teacher, what large stones and what large buildings!' Then Jesus asked him, 'Do you see these great buildings? Not one stone will be left here upon another; all will be thrown down.'" As we know from Joseph and others, the destruction of the temple was also foretold by others at that time. They had an example from the Old Testament, the prophet Jeremiah, about whom I have more to say later. (Luke 19:43; Mark 13:1)

In the words of Luke, around the time of the Passover that year, Jesus "set his face" to go to Jerusalem as a prophet. This version is confirmed by many other passages. The message Jesus would bring there was that the temple must be destroyed and that in this his own life was at stake. The cleansing of the temple was the climax. It was a prophetic action resembling what we have heard about the ancient prophets. (Jeremiah 19:1; 27:2)

The purposeful behavior of Jesus was indeed eloquent: He "began to drive out those who were selling and those who were buying in the temple, and he overturned the tables of the money changers and the seats of those who sold doves." The action was directed against the commerce related to the temple. In order to put money into the collection box, one had to change Roman money for special coins. Doves were the sacrificial animals of ordinary folk. Jesus violently opposed the whole business. According to a report in John, he even used a whip. (Mark 11:15; John 2:15)

But Jesus went even further. He explained his behavior by means of two passages from the prophets: "He was teaching and saying, 'Is it not written, "My house shall be called a house of prayer for all the nations"? But you have made it a den of robbers!'" Jeremiah fulminated against the leaders who enriched themselves at the expense of the people while saying beautiful prayers in the temple—a desecration of God's "house," which "is called by my name." (Mark 11:17; Isaiah 56:7; Jeremiah 7:11)

Jesus' deepest intention becomes clear from a detail that only Mark reports: "He would not allow anyone to carry anything through the temple." This concurs with a rabbinic prohibition to carry goods across the temple mount in order to avoid making a detour. Apparently the regulation existed already in Jesus' time, but it was not strictly followed. The motivation for the rule is to prevent a lack of respect for the temple, that is, for the one whose gracious presence in this building was presumed. We can thus understand Jesus' indignant behavior. He attached paramount significance to the holiness of the temple.

From the response to Jesus' action, it becomes clear that this was a profound conflict: "When the chief priests and the scribes heard it, they kept looking for a way to kill him; for they were afraid of him, because the whole crowd was spellbound by his teaching." The chief priests formed an elite who derived large benefits from the temple commerce. People, of course, knew this. Rabbinic literature also criticizes their greediness. They nonetheless had the support of the Roman administration. Already in Jesus' time the signs of revolt were not to be discounted. The support of the people for Jesus' action is revealing. The small but powerful priestly group had the reputation of being very cruel in jurisdiction and did not worry about one execution more or less. Jesus could not have missed this. (Mark 11:18)

That was how the cards lay. From the moment that he headed toward Jerusalem, Jesus began to speak of his death. These reports are now put in a new perspective. Jesus was deeply concerned about the desecration of the temple. What took place there was intolerable. This could not but lead to violence, war, and destruction. The only action that could be undertaken against this was to protest, as the biblical prophets had done, even though this meant risking one's life. Jesus himself felt personally called to do just that. It was his final summons to the priestly elite in Jerusalem to turn toward God's coming kingdom. The saying that he taught his disciples is applicable here: "Those who want to save their life will lose it, and those who lose their life for the sake of the gospel shall save it." (Mark 8:35, textual variant)

The Last Supper

The best-known expression of Jesus' awareness of a calling occurs in the so-called institution of the last supper. The liturgy of the ages has kept this alive, and as such it is loaded with significance. Especially here it is essential to distinguish Jesus' own intention from later adaptations.

Our oldest document is the first letter of Paul to the Corinthians. He wrote that he had already taught them the pertinent words of Jesus, which he himself had received by tradition. The epistle can be dated quite precisely: 51 or 52 c.e. The tradition that Paul had received goes back possibly another ten years. That brings us to about ten years after the supper itself—not such a long time for a final memory of a beloved master. The phrasing that Paul uses agrees strikingly with that of the first three Gospels, which here form an independent source. The differences are understandable in the framework of oral transmission. The tradition is hereby quite well attested. In Paul's version "Jesus on the night when he was betrayed took a loaf of bread, and when he had given thanks, he broke it and said, 'This is my body that is for you. . . .' In the same way he took the cup also, after supper, saying, 'This cup is the new covenant in my blood. . . .'" According to the first three Gospels, the final meal was a Jewish Passover. (1 Corinthians 11:23; Mark 14:12)

This tradition indicates that Jesus on that evening interpreted his imminent death as a self-sacrifice for his followers. It is thus presumed, first, that he foresaw his death. The preceding section makes that conceivable. Second, it is supposed that the death of a person can count as an "offering." Although it is often said that this is an un-Jewish thought, at least for Jesus' time that is not valid. There is, for example, a tradition according to which Isaac actually died upon the altar, and his death is compared to the Passover sacrifice. The tradition can be found both in the ancient Jewish *Book of Jubilees* (approximately second century B.C.E.) and in rabbinic literature. (p. 47)

These data fit well into the whole of the proceeding. I mentioned above that the heavenly voice called Jesus "My Son, the Beloved" at a turning point in his ministry and that in this is an echo of the story of Isaac. In the Christian Easter liturgy since the second century, a clear link has been made between Jesus' death, the Passover sacrifice, and the "offering" of Isaac. This tradition could go back to the direct milieu of Jesus, perhaps to Jesus himself. The oldest indication comes from 1 Corinthians. In a passage that deals with something entirely different, Paul suddenly switches to this theme, which was apparently assumed to be familiar: "For our paschal lamb, Christ, has been sacrificed." At the beginning of the 50s the tradition of viewing Jesus' death as a Passover sacrifice had apparently already taken hold. Again, the initial stages of this tradition could go back to Jesus himself. (1 Corinthians 5:7)

Finally, a more general remark: We here encounter the transition between *Jesus' own view* of his life and death and *that of his disciples*. As noted above, earlier theology assumed a breach between the belief of Jesus and that of his first followers, as well as one between Jesus and the Jews. I have argued that both assumptions are neither necessary nor correct. This is now confirmed. We can understand how the later conception of Jesus could have developed from his own teachings. The resurrection from the dead was an important part of this, and to that I shall return. (pp. 11, 80)

5

Jesus' Trial

The arrest, trial, and execution of Jesus occupy much of the biblical Gospels—approximately half of Mark and John. The "passion narrative," as it is called, assumed a prominent place in Christian tradition from the beginning. Much attention has been given to the significance we should attribute to this, a fundamental theme that I discuss elsewhere. Here I am concerned with the *fact* that Jesus was executed on a cross.

Jesus was not simply crucified; he was first tried and condemned by Jewish and Roman authorities. This means that the respective roles of these two groups in the trial must be examined. To this end I first discuss some critical issues about our sources: (1) What sources do we have, and how do they stand in relation to the parties in the case? (2) How was Jesus viewed by his Jewish contemporaries? (3) What role do the Pharisees play? (4) Who were Jesus' enemies? With these questions answered, I then attempt to reconstruct the judicial procedures.

The Sources and Their Pro-Roman Tendency

For the actual course of the proceedings we are dependent on the four Gospels. I discussed the general relationship between them in chapter 2 above and must now elaborate. In their passion narratives, as elsewhere, Matthew and Luke build upon Mark. Besides this, Luke gives the impression of having drawn from another, otherwise unknown document. The portions in Luke that do not occur in Mark or that diverge strongly from it can therefore be considered to represent an independent source. John represents its own particular tradition, whose quality is not consistent. Because this Gospel exhibits clear traces of a later redaction, it is unsuitable as a point of departure for a historical reconstruction. Nonetheless, it occasionally provides valuable historical details. Somewhat the same can be said of Matthew.

There is yet another source concerning Jesus' trial: a brief mention in the Talmud. This was written relatively late and could have undergone various adaptations. We can therefore use it only as a supplementary source. It reports that Jesus "was hanged on the evening before the Sabbath, on the eve of Passover." It is also implied that Jesus was condemned to death by an official session of the high court in Jerusalem. Both facts are of consequence to us. (Babylonian Talmud, *Sanhedrin 43a*, Florence ms.)

For our reconstruction of Jesus' arrest and trial, we thus take Mark and the divergent or inserted portions in Luke as a starting point. These two sources can be cautiously supplemented by trustworthy details from Matthew, John, and the report in the Talmud.

The position our sources assume in regard to the parties involved in the trial needs to be clarified. In particular, what role is given to the Roman and Jewish authorities? On this, the sources appear to be colored—not to say prejudiced—to various degrees. This is quite understandable; for those involved, everything culminated at this point. It was a life-or-death matter:"Whoever is not for us is against us." In such a situation it was difficult to repress the tendency toward polarization.

First, a few more facts. Crucifixion as a method of execution was not invented by the Romans, but they used it with a vengeance, especially for rebels and insubordinate slaves. This was one of the cruel aspects of their rule. In particular the fact that the executed often remained for days in the throes of death was an atrocity. This weighed the more heavily for Jews, who took seriously the biblical rule that an executed one may not remain hanging overnight, because "anyone hanging on a tree is under

God's curse." Humankind is, after all, created in God's image. This is true of a criminal, and even more so of a condemned one who is innocent. (Deuteronomy 21:23; Galatians 3:13)

Roman authority was represented in Jesus' time by the governor, Pontius Pilate. Josephus and other sources describe him as a cruel administrator with little respect for the Jews. The same impression is given by an isolated report in Luke. Pilate had once let the blood of certain Galileans be "mingled with their sacrifices"; he had them slaughtered while they were offering in the temple. (Luke 13:1)

All of this would lead us to expect that the Roman administration would play a disinterested role in the passion story—but such was not the case. Pilate is depicted as cautious and, at most, somewhat indulgent toward Jesus' accusers. Almost everywhere he is absolved of guilt. In Luke he says *three times* that he sees no reason to condemn Jesus. In Matthew he even literally washes his hands to announce his innocence. In John Pilate is impressed that Jesus is called God's Son, and he wants to release him. Only in Mark is the behavior of Pilate described fairly neutrally. What is going on here? (Luke 23; John 18–19; Matthew 27:24; Deuteronomy 21:6; Mark 15)

We must keep in mind that all of the biblical Gospels appear to be written for non-Jewish Christians during or after the first war with Rome. At that time, outsiders often still linked Christianity to the Jews. In the climate of war, however, relations between the Jews and the non-Jewish Christians had deteriorated. The position of the Jews within the Roman Empire had been affected as well. It became logical for non-Jewish Christians to distance themselves from the Jews and to seek the favor of the Romans. That the evangelists minimize the responsibility of the Roman authorities for the execution is thus understandable. The more neutral nature of the account in Mark fits with a possibly somewhat older dating of the Gospel.

The exoneration of the Romans naturally arouses the suspicion that our sources have shifted the blame to the Jews. We therefore need to observe how the Jewish authorities are presented. In order to do that convincingly, we first take inventory of how Jesus was viewed by his Jewish contemporaries.

Supporters and Doubters

According to all the Gospels, Jesus had a multitude of supporters outside of the circle of his disciples. These were primarily to be found among the ordinary people. Repeatedly we read of an unnamed "crowd" or multitude that was drawn to him and accompanied him during his entire ministry. According to the reports, these people continually brought along the sick, with whom Jesus often was occupied until late at night. Wherever he arrived, the whole village immediately congregated; a house that he might enter would become crammed. At times he had to take to a boat to speak to the multitude on the shore. It is also reported that once in the open fields at the end of the day there were several thousand without food. Even from Jerusalem and from the Jewish homeland across the Jordan, people came to Galilee to listen to him. (Mark 1:33; 2:2; 3:8; 4:1; 6:35)

On the journey to Jerusalem the multitude was present. It accompanied Jesus on his travels through the Jewish homeland across the Jordan and through Jericho, from where the road ascended to the Holy City. At that moment Jerusalem was full of pilgrims from far and near who had come to celebrate the Jewish Passover. According to the reports, Jesus rode into the city on a donkey, and the throng welcomed him not only by singing the customary verse from the Psalms, "Blessed is the one who comes in the name of the Lord!" but also by greeting him as the son of David, the coming Messiah. (Mark 10–11; Psalm 118:26; John 12:12)

Even if these accounts are exaggerated, an immense positive interest is apparent among the common people. They were attracted to Jesus' preaching and acts of healing—in other words, to his gospel, his good news of God's coming dominion. We have seen that Jesus' disciples reported that the people saw him as the promised prophet and deliverer. In those days, messianic expectations hung in the air. It was only natural for this expectation to be heightened around Passover, the feast commemorating the deliverance from Egypt.

In Jerusalem Jesus came to a fatal clash with the authorities. Here again, however, we encounter the multitude of Jewish sympathizers—who even played a strategic role. When Jesus took action against the commerce in the temple, the alarmed temple administration intervened. This became the precursor to his arrest and trial. The people, however, were fascinated by Jesus' teachings. Days on end they were "spellbound by his teaching." According to the accounts, this made the authorities powerless, and they took recourse to cunning. When Jesus was led away to be executed, again a large throng accompanied him, lamenting. (Mark 11:18; 12:12; Luke 19:38; 21:38; 23:27; John 12:19)

Besides the anonymous multitude of ordinary people, there were important sympathizers whose names are mentioned. All the Gospels report the rich Joseph from Arimathea, "a respected member of the council," who came to bury Jesus. Mark adds that "he was also himself waiting expectantly for the kingdom of God," a remark that Luke adopts. Matthew and John interpret this to mean that he "was also a [secret] disciple" of Jesus. We observe here the creation of Christian legends that make disciples of sympathizers. Something similar occurs with Gamaliel—and even with Pilate in later apocryphal Gospels. Regarding the burial, John mentions also Joseph's fellow council member, the scholar of the law Nicodemus. According to this Gospel, he had defended Jesus when the other temple administrators were plotting against him. Nicodemus now brought costly ointment for the burial. With the exception of the creation of legends already noted, these accounts contradict the tendency to blame Jewish agencies, and thus make a trustworthy impression. (Mark 15:43; Matthew 27:57; Luke 23:50; John 3:1; 7:50; 19:38)

There were also many Jews who had doubts concerning Jesus. There must have been many more of these than our sources report. Without question, the supporters formed a small minority, and we shall see that this also was true of the hard-core enemies. Between these two extremes there must have been many Jews who could not or would not decide for or against Jesus. Something similar is reported about no less than his former teacher, John the Baptist. According to the account, John from prison sent messengers to ask Jesus whether he was the "one who is to come" or not. This speaks volumes. John had much in common with Jesus, and he had no trouble assuming a divergent standpoint. Nonetheless, he was uncertain about Jesus. (Matthew 11:2; Luke 7:19; p. 35)

Initially, Jesus' relatives doubted as well. His brother James later became the leader of the Jerusalem church. Letters in the New Testament are ascribed to him and his younger brother Jude. These men rose to prominence among Jesus' followers, but in the beginning this was not so. The Gospels give the impression that Jesus' relatives at first did feel attracted to his preaching but remained at a distance. They knew him too well and therefore could not take his message fully seriously. The distance was mutual; Jesus did not see his gospel as a family matter. (Galatians 1:19; Acts 12:17; Mark 3:31; 6:3; John 7:3)

Doubts were present as well with those more removed from Jesus. For example, certain Pharisees were sent with a question to Jesus in the temple. It was a dangerous question: Should taxes be paid to the Roman emperor or not? Given his criticism of riches and power, Jesus could hardly say yes, but to say no would reek of revolt. His answer was astonishing. He asked what appeared on a Roman coin. The image of the emperor, they replied. "Give to the emperor the things that are the emperor's," he said, "and to God the things that are God's." It is assumed that the reader will recall the statement in Genesis that human beings bear God's image. According to rabbinic literature, this awareness was also fundamental in the thinking of the Pharisees. Thus Jesus killed two birds with one stone: he placed obedience to God uppermost without denying obedience to the emperor. According to the conclusion of the account, the Pharisaic inquirers were "utterly amazed at him." (Mark 12:17; Matthew 22:22; Genesis 1:26)

On another occasion Jesus surprised a scholar of the law who asked which commandment summarized the whole law of Moses. Jesus took two commandments that begin with the same word and connected them: "*Love* the Lord your God with all your heart," and "*love* your neighbor as yourself." According to the account in Mark, the inquirer agreed enthusiastically, and Jesus said that he was "not far from the kingdom of God." The bystanders dared not ask anything further. The concurrence between Jesus and the scribe is not coincidental. Not only was the question a Pharisaic topic of discussion, as I mentioned above, but Jesus' answer also confirmed their spiritual affinity. The announcement in Matthew that this scribe was also a Pharisee therefore sounds plausible. (Mark 12:28; p. 31)

These two reports about the Pharisees suggest that they were sympathetic to Jesus but that they kept themselves at a distance. This hesitation appears not to be an isolated incident. There are other similar reports, especially in Luke and even in John. (John 9:16)

These reports also agree with the impression we get from other sources. Jesus showed affinity to the Pharisees and shared their insights on many points. In other respects, he thought much more radically than most of them did. According to rabbinic tradition, the Pharisees were for moderation and level-headedness. According to them, differences of opinion should not lead to termination of fellowship. In contrast, Jesus had a radical attitude on social issues such as money and possessions. His summons to baptism as a conversion in view of the imminent kingdom of God was a radical message that implied joining a type of spiritual community. The most debated point was probably the one about which John the Baptist also expressed doubts: Jesus' conviction that he played a key role in the messianic future. Jesus thus shared important presuppositions with the Pharisees, while on other points he assumed a more radical attitude. This explains the Pharisees' doubts. Many were sympathetic to Jesus but kept their distance from his radical message.

The doubts remained. A prominent example is Gamaliel, known from the Talmud as a leader from the school of Hillel. The book of Acts reports that he advocated leaving Jesus' apostles alone when they were accused by the high priest. His answer reflects typical Pharisaic wisdom. Humans cannot determine whether Jesus' message and that of his apostles were inspired by God: "If this plan or this undertaking is of human origin, it will fail; but if it is of God, you will not be able to overthrow them." The same wise attitude is expressed in several sayings in rabbinic literature. (Acts 5:34)

Further on in Acts, in the lawsuit against Paul, the Pharisaic council members again assume a sensible attitude, revealing a certain amount of sympathy, but also distance. The apocryphal tradition that represents Gamaliel as a crypto-Christian is certainly incorrect. Nonetheless, we do read of Pharisees who joined Jesus' movement. One of these is known to us from his own writings—Paul. According to the same source, he was a former pupil of Gamaliel. (Acts 15:5; 23:9; p. 59)

This information about Pharisaic hesitancy between sympathy for and distance from Jesus is noteworthy. It contradicts the tendency to blame Jesus' death not on the Romans but on the Jewish authorities. With this background, I now compare the role of the Pharisees in the various passion narratives.

The Pharisees in the Passion Narratives

In *Mark*'s passion narrative the Pharisees take action but once, when the temple authorities send "some Pharisees and some Herodians" to Jesus with the question about imperial taxes. Herodians were members of Herod's court. Along with certain Pharisees they were deployed to pose a trick question. The group, however, was impressed by Jesus' answer! (Mark 11:27; 12:13)

In the passion story in *Luke*, the Pharisees appear once as well, but at an entirely different point. When Jesus rode into the city on a donkey and was welcomed as a king, "Some of the Pharisees in the crowd said to him, 'Teacher, order your disciples to stop.'" They were afraid that the matter would get out of hand. Concern rather than enmity is reflected. (Luke 19:39)

This is not to say that there were no Pharisees opposed to Jesus. Here again Paul is our best example, although this could be because of our lack of information. Both Paul himself and the book of Acts report that, as a young Pharisee, he was a passionate opponent of Jesus' followers. The book of Acts relates as well that many synagogues resisted Jesus' message; in this Pharisaic motives would have played a role. The conclusion is the more convincing: except for the two interventions mentioned, the Pharisees play no role in the story of Jesus' trial in Luke or in Mark.

In this *Matthew* diverges strongly. Here the question about imperial taxes was not initiated by the chief priests but only by the Pharisees. Nonetheless, again the Pharisaic inquirers were surprised at Jesus' response! This gives the impression that the antagonistic initiative of the Pharisees was inserted by the evangelist. The phrasing as well points to a later addition. (Matthew 22:15)

Deviating from Mark, subsequently in Matthew it is the Pharisees who gathered together to ask Jesus about the greatest commandment. There is no trace of the harmony with which the passage ends in Mark. Then, in Matthew alone, Jesus posed a counter-question to the gathered Pharisees. We thus observe in Matthew a foundational contrast between Jesus and the Pharisees. This is clearly the case in the lengthy judgmental discourse against the scribes and Pharisees that follows immediately in Matthew 23. It takes up a whole chapter and is inserted into the Markan sequence. Again and again comes the refrain, "Woe to you, scribes and

Pharisees, hypocrites. . . ." The contents also point to a later reworking in a more hostile climate, for in a number of important points Jesus appears to agree with the "hypocrites"! (Matthew 22:34; 23:1)

More remarkable yet is the fact that Matthew goes on to associate the Pharisees with the chief priests. As we shall see, the latter were the true enemies of Jesus. According to Mark and Luke, Jesus told the chief priests a parable about tenant farmers who forfeit their tenancy. In Matthew, however, we read, "When the chief priests *and the Pharisees* heard his parables . . . they wanted to arrest him, but they feared the crowds. . . ." The Pharisees are placed over against the people and on the side of Jesus' enemies. The same occurs in a strange report at the end. When Jesus lay in the grave, the "chief priests *and the Pharisees*" organized a guard at the tomb. When they later were informed that the body was gone, they said that the disciples had stolen it. The evangelist adds, "And this story is still told among the Jews to this day." This clearly attests to a later reworking of the material. (Matthew 21:45; 27:62; 28:11)

The *Gospel of John* stands completely by itself. There is no earlier text with which to compare it. Nonetheless, it is immediately clear that the relationships are entirely different from what they are in Mark and Luke. The Pharisees are repeatedly involved in plans to kill Jesus. They appear in such a context five times alongside the chief priests, both previous to and during the passion narrative. (John 5:18; 7:32, 45; 11:47; 12:19; 18:3)

Even more strongly than Matthew, John places the Pharisees next to the hostile chief priests, while the people stand behind Jesus. Furthermore, in John all opponents of Jesus are usually simply indicated as "the Jews." Jesus and his disciples are thus depicted at a remarkable distance from the Jews, as though they themselves were not Jews. This is indicative of a later situation in which the Jews were viewed as enemies of Jesus.

The conclusion is clear: the passion narratives of Matthew and John are prejudiced against the Pharisees. Taking Mark and Luke as the starting point for historical understanding is hereby confirmed.

Jesus' Enemies

Jesus had not only sympathizers and doubters but also real enemies. Who these were comes out clearly during his action in the temple. In Mark we read: "And when the *chief priests and the scribes* heard it, they kept looking for a way to kill him; for they were afraid of him, because the whole crowd was spellbound by his teaching." In Luke we read, "The *chief priests, the scribes,* and the leaders of the people kept looking for a way to kill him; but they did not find anything they could do, for all the people were spellbound by what they heard." In Matthew as well, Jesus ran into these authorities in the temple. (Mark 11:18; Luke 19:47; Matthew 21:45)

Who were these enemies? The term *scribes* has been mentioned already. They did not constitute a particular party but were clerks or functionaries, sometimes linked to the Pharisees. In the context of the temple, they were bookkeepers or administrators, usually in the retinue of the *chief priests.* We have observed that according to Matthew Jesus gave the "scribes and Pharisees" a stern dressing-down in the temple. The composition of this tirade betrays the evangelist's hand. The same is true as well of the expression "scribes and Pharisees" itself. (Mark 2:16; Luke 5:30; Acts 23:9; p. 62)

Luke also mentions the *leaders of the people,* nonpriests who occupied a public position—for example, members of the council. In antiquity, these were always rich people, for public positions were not remunerated. In Old Testament terminology they were also called *elders,* which is how they appear in the passion narratives. These also did not belong to one party. Due to their social position, they would often have felt at home with the chief priests. But not all would have: we already have met one exception— Joseph of Arimathea. (p. 59)

Foremost among Jesus' enemies were the *chief priests.* According to the Old Testament, priests were all descendants of the male line of Aaron, Moses' brother. In Jesus' time they comprised twenty-four divisions that served in the temple in turn. Most lived among the people and had a trade. There were, however, also several rich and powerful priestly families. From their midst the *high priest* was chosen, the most prominent religious leader, who also presided over the high court. Rabbinic literature preserves bitter reports about the manner in which they misused their power at the expense of ordinary priests, for example, by confiscating the hides of the sacrificial animals that were allotted to the priests. In the New Testament, the members of these families are designated "chief priests." (Exodus 28:1; 1 Chronicles 24:1; Luke 1:5)

The name *Sadducees* is derived from the priestly name Zadok and indicates a party or lobby that largely coincided with the chief priests and their followers. In the Acts of the Apostles this group is described in so many words:" . . . the high priest . . . and all who were with him (that is, the sect of the Sadducees)." There they play a significant role: they had Jesus' apostles arrested. Later Paul also had to face them. On that occasion Acts reports that they would have nothing to do with ideas such as angels and the resurrection of the dead. This concurs with facts known from other sources. According to the Talmud, the Pharisee Gamaliel, whom we have already met, disputed with them on this matter. The same is related of Jesus, to whom the Sadducees posed a trick question on the topic. It is not conceivable that they could have had ears for his gospel of the coming kingdom for the poor. (Acts 5:17; 23:8; Mark 12:18)

This party is described more extensively at another clash with Jesus' apostles: "While Peter and John [Greek: they] were speaking to the people, *the priests, the captain of the temple, and the Sadducees* came to them, much annoyed because they were teaching the people and proclaiming that in Jesus there is the resurrection of the dead. . . . The next day their rulers, *elders,* and *scribes* assembled in Jerusalem, with Annas the *high priest,* Caiaphas, John, and Alexander and all who were of the *high-priestly family.*" (Acts 4:1)

In this connection mention should be made of the *Sanhedrin,* the high court under the leadership of the high priest, which met in the temple compound. The name comes from the Greek word *synhedrion,* "session" or official council meeting. In rabbinic Hebrew, this became *sanhedrin.* The high court decided difficult cases, questions having to do with the calendar, and penal cases involving the death sentence. According to Acts, both Sadducees and Pharisees were members of the high court. Joseph of Arimathea was a member of the council but is mentioned neither as a priest nor as a Pharisee. Nicodemus was a member of the council and a Pharisee. Neither of the two were enemies of Jesus. Both Jesus and his apostles were examined by the Sanhedrin. (Acts 23:7)

Acts in particular gives us clear information about the relationships. Opposing Jesus' followers we consistently find the party of the chief priests, scribes, and elders—in other words, the high priest and his followers or the Sadducees. Josephus reports that the execution of James,

Jesus' brother, was instigated by this group as well. This was in 62 c.e. The "most authoritative interpreters of the law"—apparently the Phari-sees—protested.

Jesus' sworn enemies were thus the high priest, the chief priests, and their followers. The animosity was reciprocal. As we saw in the preceding chapter, the cleansing of the temple was an intentional conflict with this priestly elite. Jesus could not have been ignorant of their reputation of harshness. It is even probable that he took into account the possibility of being killed as a result of this confrontation. We have looked at the bibli-cal themes he could have related to this. (p. 50)

The temple authorities were the ones who formally thwarted him: "As he was walking in the temple, the chief priests, the scribes, and the elders came to him and said, 'By *what authority* are you doing these things? Who gave you this authority to do them?' Jesus said to them, 'I will ask you one question; answer me, and I will tell you by what authority I do these things. Did the baptism of John come from heaven, or was it of human origin?'" The authorities did not dare reveal their opinion, for the mul-titude unanimously supported the Baptist, and Jesus knew this. It was not the *Pharisees* who posed this question about Jesus' authority. This concurs with their cautious, rather hesitant attitude toward divine truth. The question was posed by the high priest and his cohorts, the temple authorities. According to Acts, they later asked the same question of Jesus' apostles. (Mark 11:27; Luke 20:1; Matthew 12:23; Acts 4:1; p. 61)

Jesus assumed the offensive and challenged the authority of the chief priests. He told a parable of tenants who refused to pay the rent for the vineyard. The tenants molested the servants of the owner and killed his son. In the end, the owner evicted them and gave the vineyard to others. Jesus' message was clear: he did not accept the greedy temple administra-tion and foretold that when God's kingdom comes, they would lose their power. They would hear none of it: "When they realized that he had told this parable against them, they wanted to arrest him, but they feared the crowd." Again it is clear to what extent the people stood behind Jesus. This agrees with reports in the writings of the rabbis and from Qumran that criticize the Jerusalem chief priests. (Mark 12:12; Luke 20:19)

These then are the positions taken toward Jesus and how our sources treat them. The people supported Jesus, the Pharisees doubted, and the temple authorities were hostile. This is to be concluded from Mark and Luke, supplemented by other sources. Matthew introduces a later aggravation of the positions by counting also the Pharisees among Jesus' enemies. John does the same, and exacerbates the matter further by lumping all enemies together as "the Jews." I therefore confidently take Mark and the special material in Luke as my point of departure for the reconstruction of the trial and fit individual details from other sources into this.

The Trial by the Sanhedrin

The legal proceedings took place in two phases: first a trial by the Jewish authorities, that is, by the Sanhedrin, and then a trial by the Romans. We begin with the first phase.

Initially, Jesus' opponents conceived of a plan: "It was two days before the Passover and the festival of Unleavened Bread. The chief priests and the scribes were looking for a way to arrest Jesus by stealth and kill him; for they said, 'Not during the feast, or there may be a riot among the people.'" Matthew adds to this company the high priest Caiaphas, who is also known from other sources. Jesus' disciple Judas is drawn into the plan. By his help, the arrest in Gethsemane, a garden on the Mount of Olives, took place in the evening, after the Passover meal. According to Mark, Judas came with an armed unit sent by "the chief priests, the scribes, and the elders." Luke calls it a company of "chief priests, the officers of the temple police, and the elders." (Mark 14:1, 32; Luke 22:2, 39; Matthew 26:4, 36)

Our sources diverge considerably concerning the trial that follows. Mark reports extensively on an interrogation at night at the high priest's house, which he calls a *synhedrion*. At this nocturnal gathering, the high priest and "all the chief priests, the elders, and the scribes" were present. They sought grounds for an accusation, but the witnesses contradicted one another. Then "the high priest asked him, 'Are you the Messiah, the son of the Blessed One?' Jesus said, 'I am,'" and continued with a saying about the Son of Man coming on the clouds. Upon this, the high priests and his cohorts condemned him to death. When it became day, they called an official meeting, also called *synhedrion*. It was decided to deliver Jesus to

Pilate, by which the verdict apparently was confirmed. The Pharisees are not mentioned. (Mark 14:53; 15:1)

As a check, we take a look at Matthew and John. Matthew follows Mark but is more concise. Jesus' answer to the question of whether he was the Messiah is given differently: "You have said so." Here again no Pharisees are mentioned in connection with the trial. But in John, they are involved. There the decision to kill Jesus was taken earlier at a session of the *synhedrion* where Jesus himself was not heard. The meeting was at the initiative of the "chief priests and the Pharisees." Together these also made the arrest. In both cases these opponents are called "the Jews." In John as well, after Jesus' arrest there was an interrogation at night before the high priest, but there was no ensuing morning session, and Jesus was brought to Pilate without a decision. We clearly see here the tendency to blame the Jewish authorities, and we are not given a consistent account about the procedure followed. (Matthew 26:64; John 11:47; 18:1, 14)

In contrast, the alternative course of events portrayed by Luke is significant to our reconstruction. Here again Jesus was apprehended in the evening and brought to the high priest's house, but no interrogation followed. Only when day had dawned did "the assembly of the elders of the people, both chief priests and scribes" convene, and they brought him "to their council (*synhedrion*)." During the ensuing questioning, they asked him first whether he was the Messiah. He gave an evasive answer, but then seemed to affirm the question indirectly by a saying about the "Son of Man [who] will be seated at right hand of the power of God." When they then asked whether he was God's son, Jesus answered as in Matthew: "You say that I am." The temple authorities took this as grounds for the death sentence. (Luke 22:66)

The essential difference between Mark and Luke lies in the description of the procedure. Mark tells twice of a formal *synhedrion*, one at night and one in the morning. The term is fitting for the morning session, which appears to be intended to formalize an improvised decision. It is doubtful whether it also is appropriate for the nocturnal examination. Luke, in contrast, reports no interrogation at night and relates only a *synhedrion* in the morning. This presents us with two difficulties. The first has to do with the *time* of the session, namely, in the evening and/or the daytime. Another problem involved in the descriptions of Mark and Luke lies behind this: the *date* of the session on Passover.

Date and Time of the Session

The crucial question involves the specific conditions under which a session counted as valid. It might be that the various parties had differently views on this question. A number of rabbinic regulations reveal what the issue was. Trials involving a death sentence must be held and completed *during the daytime*. Before the death sentence could be pronounced, a night must go by: "Therefore one does not pass judgment on the eve of the Sabbath or of feast days"—for on the Sabbath and on feast days themselves, no judgment may be passed. In their present form, these regulations were written down in the third century, but their essence could be several centuries older, for they also contain stipulations that concern the temple, which was destroyed in 70 c.e. Furthermore, Philo of Alexandria was familiar with the prohibition of passing judgment on the Sabbath. It is therefore probable that at least some of the Pharisees in Jesus' time adhered to a basic form of these regulations. (Mishnah, *Sanhedrin* 4:1)

The issue, then, is whether there actually could have been a valid trial. According to Mark and Luke, the matter was decided on the day after Jesus had held the Passover meal, that is, on the first day of the feast. This would be in flagrant conflict with rabbinic and possibly also Pharisaic regulations. It is known that in this matter the Sadducees were stricter than the Pharisees. They were opposed, for example, to waving palm branches on the Sabbath during the Feast of Booths, something the Pharisees did allow. The chief priests and their scribes more often than not were Sadducees. A trial on the first day of Passover is therefore practically excluded. From this some scholars draw the radical conclusion that there was no valid trial. Such a conclusion, however, conflicts with the general impression gained from all the sources, including the account in the Talmud. It is more probable that our chief sources contain inner contradictions. They report a trial, but on an incorrect date.

At this point, John's account is important. Independently of Mark and Luke, this Gospel gives another dating of the trial. According to John's passion narrative, Jesus was handed over to Pilate by the chief priests and was crucified on the day *before* the Passover. This dating is furthermore confirmed by the report in the Talmud: "Jesus the Nazarene was hanged on the eve of the Sabbath, *on the eve of Passover*." John's account, however, presents another difficulty: here Jesus' last supper could not have been the Jewish Passover meal. Indeed, the evangelist explicitly states that the meal occurred "before the festival of the Passover." This in turn contradicts the report from our main sources, which explicitly speak of a Passover meal. (John 13:1; 19:31; Mark 14:12; Luke 22:15; p. 31)

Many scholars assume that the discrepancies in our sources cannot be resolved—as indeed would be the case were it not that the Jews of that time followed *different calendars*. Such has been definitely confirmed by the Qumran scrolls. According to the calendar found there, the feasts at Qumran occurred on different days than they did at the temple in Jerusalem. Apparently Jesus also celebrated the feast according to some such divergent calendar, which is several days earlier than in the temple. Mark and Luke follow this alternative calendar. According to them, Jesus' last supper and his trial occurred on the Jewish Passover. In the temple, the feast was celebrated later, and that is the calendar followed by John. In John, Jesus' last supper, trial, and crucifixion all occurred before the Passover in the temple. At that time the difference between the two calendars was apparently four days. Both Mark and John report that Jesus was anointed by a woman before the Passover feast in Bethany. In Mark this is dated *two* days before the feast, in John *six*—with equal emphasis in both. (Mark 14:1; John 12:1)

Not many scholars accept the solution offered here. Nonetheless, this is a natural explanation of the contradictions in our main sources, and it cancels the doubt about the possibility of a valid trial.

We return to the question of the *time* of the court session. According to Mark, the trial began in the evening; according to Luke, it was completed within one day. Rabbinic regulations stipulate that a death sentence can only be pronounced when a case is begun in the daytime and settled at least one day later. We cannot determine how many Pharisees of that day adhered to these rules. It is immensely significant, however, that our main sources do not mention Pharisees at all in connection with the trial. Did the Pharisees boycott the trial? Luke says that Joseph of Arimathea, a member of the court, "had not agreed to their plan and action," but Luke does not say whether Joseph was a Pharisee. In contrast, from John it appears that the council member Nicodemus was a Pharisee, but that he had no part in such a decision. We can safely conclude with certainty that not all Pharisees could have endorsed the procedure followed. (Luke 23:51; John 7:50)

We have scant information on what the Sadducees and the chief priests thought on this issue. Our sources, however, provide a little insight. According to both accounts, Mark and Luke, the chief priests took care that the *pronouncement* was made in the morning session. They, too, apparently thought that a death sentence should be delivered in the daytime. A trial in one day, or in a night and a day, was apparently valid in the opinion of the Sadducees and chief priests, and perhaps according to some Pharisees as well.

The Verdict

Finally, we consider the grounds for the death sentence. Both of our main sources relate that this followed from the question put to Jesus whether he was the Messiah and Son of God. In Mark he gave a straight answer: "I am." Considering the evasive responses found in Luke and Matthew, that sounds rather improbable. In any event, with his statement about the coming Son of Man, Jesus confirmed indirectly that he saw himself as the Son of God as well (for the biblical and Jewish backgrounds of the expression Son of Man, see above). The chief priests in Jerusalem could not bear to hear such language. Presumably they thought like the Sadducees, who would have nothing to do with angels, revelations, and the resurrection of the dead. (p. 29)

For the chief priests, Jesus' guilt was hereby settled. Mark mentions the accusation: *blasphemy*. They viewed Jesus as a blasphemer and a false prophet who, according to the law of Moses, should be put to death. In hindsight, the decisive significance of their question at the beginning— on what authority Jesus was acting—becomes apparent. There was also another side to the case, namely, Jesus' protest against their greed and disrespect, while the people supported him. In this they rightly felt a threat to their social position. However that may be, the chief priests would have nothing of Jesus' gospel of God's kingdom that was coming for the poor. Thus they revealed themselves to be literally Jesus' mortal enemies. This could hardly have come as a surprise to Jesus. (Deuteronomy 18:20; Leviticus 24:16; p. 67)

The Trial by Pilate

The second phase of the process assumes the verdict of the first, the death sentence by the Jewish authorities. As indicated, the trial comes to a climax before Pilate and involves the question of who was finally responsible for Jesus' execution.

Again I start with our primary sources. The tale in Mark is straightforward. The accusation with which Jesus was handed over to Pilate is not stated. Pilate, however, appeared to be informed, and he asked Jesus whether he was "the King of the Jews." Jesus gave him no answer, which surprised Pilate. After the readers are told that the Romans always released a Jewish prisoner at a feast, Pilate asked whether he should release "the King of the Jews." "For he realized that it was out of jealousy that the chief priests had handed him over." The crowd was manipulated to request the release of Barabbas, a political rebel. Then things moved swiftly. Pilate asked again what he should do with "the King of the Jews." They shouted for crucifixion. Pilate asked what the crime was. They cried out the more, "Crucify him!" Pilate then acceded. He had Jesus whipped and led away to be crucified. (Mark 15:2)

In Mark, the accusation comes only from the chief priests, and it was that Jesus passed himself off as the King of the Jews. This is a political rendering of the—to their ears—blasphemous pretension that he was the Messiah and the Son of God. Pilate apparently was not impressed. He was taken aback at Jesus' silence and noted the envy behind the allegation. That is to say, there was in fact no real charge. Three times he asked what they wanted: Was Jesus to be released, and if not, what must be done with him? If he must die, what was his crime? Observing this narrative objectively, we note in Pilate's behavior a sort of detached amazement, even irony, toward the obsession of the chief priests about such a relatively innocuous individual. This attitude fits well with a military governor of a people with whom he had little in common.

In all his conciseness, Luke provides valuable extra details. In order to convince Pilate, the chief priests mentioned first a threefold accusation with a political slant: "We found this man perverting our nation, forbidding us to pay taxes to the emperor, and saying that he himself is the Messiah, a king." Pilate questioned Jesus whether he was the king of the Jews, and after his evasive answer said to "the chief priests and the crowds,

'I find no basis for an accusation against this man.'" They then added new arguments: "He stirs up the people by teaching throughout all Judea, from Galilee where he began even to this place." (Luke 23:2)

The way was thus opened for the questioning by Herod Antipas. This episode is reported only in Luke and clearly belongs to material from another, unknown Gospel. Antipas was in Jerusalem for the feast, and Pilate called him in to see whether he was able to do anything with Jesus. Antipas was, after all, regent of Galilee, and Jesus thus was his subject. Besides this formal reason, Antipas came from a family of regents knowledgeable of Jewish culture and religion. The trustworthiness of this report is strengthened by the announcement that up to that time Pilate and Antipas had no dealings with one another. Antipas was curious about Jesus and was happy finally to have him to himself. Jesus, however, refused to speak, while "the chief priests and the scribes" again heaped up their accusations. Antipas reacted as though insulted. Derisively he let Jesus be clothed in a royal robe and sent him back to Pilate. (Luke 23:6)

Behind Jesus' silence toward Antipas lies a story about which we have some information. According to scattered reports in the Gospels and in Josephus, Antipas had had John the Baptist imprisoned and executed because John had openly criticized him for the manner in which he had divorced and remarried. The people greatly resented Antipas for John's execution. Jesus was not safe with Antipas either; the Pharisees had once warned him of a plot to arrest him. In his answer at that point Jesus called Antipas a fox, that sly animal from popular fables. Finally, the followers of Antipas's family, the "Herodians," are mentioned among Jesus' opponents. These stories provide interesting historical relief to the Herodian episode in Luke. (Mark 6:14; 12:13; Luke 13:31)

In Luke's passion narrative, the governor now reopened his examination: "Pilate then called together the chief priests, the leaders, and the people, and said to them, 'You brought me this man as one who was perverting the people; and here I have examined him in your presence and have not found this man guilty of any of your charges against him. Neither has Herod. . . . Indeed, he has done nothing to deserve death.'" On their own initiative, they now began to demand the release of Barabbas. Pilate raised his voice to declare that he wanted to free Jesus, but they demanded his crucifixion. "A third time he said to them, 'Why, what evil has he done? I have found in him no ground for the sentence of death.'"

They continued to shout for crucifixion, and Pilate gave in. (Luke 23:4, 13, 22)

Not only the Herod episode but also small accents make Luke's tale an interesting supplementation to Mark's. The indictment by the chief priests is more specific, which indicates the background of their hostility toward Jesus. They considered his message to be subversive, arguing that he perverted the people and called himself the Messiah, a king. According to this account, Pilate was not impressed by the latter accusation nor by their argument that Jesus incited the people not to pay taxes to the emperor. He was evidently not dangerous to Roman authority, certainly not in comparison to a character like Barabbas. It is even more clear that it was particularly the chief priests who considered Jesus dangerous.

In contrast to Mark, Luke does not give the impression that Pilate viewed the agitation with irony. He is depicted as a well-meaning Roman administrator. He did everything possible to give Jesus an honest trial and thrice explicitly asserted that he saw no basis for the death penalty. This is not congruent with the image of Pilate that we get from other sources. Thus Luke also reveals a tendency to exonerate the Romans. The author evidently had reason to take Roman sensitivity into account. It is noteworthy, however, that Luke does not proceed to augment the Jews' guilt. Just as in Mark, in Luke only the chief priests and their people are responsible for Jesus' execution. Moreover, Luke offers convincing details for this. In spite of his deference to the Romans, this author remains remarkably balanced toward the Jews.

For a comparison I consider Matthew. Here, too, Pilate is excused, even by means of a legend: "While he was sitting on the judgment seat, his wife sent word to him, 'Have nothing to do with that innocent man, for today I have suffered a great deal because of a dream about him.'" He did what he could, but without result. "So when Pilate saw that he could do nothing, but rather that a riot was beginning, he took some water and washed his hands before the crowd, saying, 'I am innocent of this man's blood; see to it yourselves.' Then the people as a whole answered, 'His blood be on us and on our children!'" (Matthew 27:19, 24)

Pilate's action strongly resembles the Old Testament ritual prescribed for a murder committed by an unknown person—an improbable gesture for a Roman administrator. It appears that the evangelist is exonerating

Pilate. The responsibility is put upon the heads of "the people as a whole." It is not clear who is intended. In the first place, just as in Mark and Luke, it is "the crowd" that was inflamed by the chief priests. We saw that Matthew includes also the Pharisees among Jesus' opponents at the temple. He does not mention them in connection with the trial but does do so after the burial of Jesus, along with the chief priests. As I will show below, Matthew contains numerous other accents that make the ominous reference to "the people as a whole" effectively sound like a self-imprecation by the Jewish people. (Deuteronomy 21:6)

Jewish enmity toward Jesus is depicted even more strongly in John. Alongside the chief priests, the Pharisees are mentioned as Jesus' mortal enemies, and subsequently they are all lumped together as "the Jews." In the negotiations with Pilate, the Pharisees are no longer mentioned; rather, the chief priests and their servants take action. They, too, are regularly called "the Jews." Pilate even seemed to develop a certain respect for Jesus. At the climax of the drama we hear the pronouncement: "*The Jews* answered him, 'We have a law, and according to that law he ought to die because he has claimed to be the Son of God'" (John 19:6, 14.)

Conclusion

Mark's report appears to be the most historically authentic regarding Pilate. Pilate was not impressed by the indictment by the chief priests and did not find Jesus dangerous to the state. He did seem to be surprised by the vehemence with which Jesus was accused. When the release of Barabbas was preferred—one who was a subversive activist—Pilate cynically gave in.

Mark and Luke concur with respect to the Jewish authorities. Jesus' death was brought about by his main enemies, the chief priests and their followers, that is, the Sadducees. They would have nothing of his preaching and felt threatened in their position, the more so because the people supported him enthusiastically. They succeeded in capturing Jesus unseen, trying him according to their tradition, and condemning him according to their convictions. His unarticulated pretension to be the heavenly Son of Man and Son of God they considered a blasphemous crime.

Jesus' execution was mourned not only by his disciples but also by many of the people. Luke provides the following depiction of Jesus on the way to Golgotha: "A great number of the people followed him, and among them were women who were beating their breasts and wailing for him." (Luke 23:27)

The Pharisees were not present. Many would have rejected both the legal proceedings and the final verdict. The same constellation is evidenced at the Sanhedrin session against Jesus' disciples and again at the interrogation of Paul about thirty years later. Because of the protest on the part of the Pharisees, these ended positively for the accused. On a fourth occasion, however, things again went wrong. When Jesus' brother James was hastily executed several years later, the Pharisees could only subsequently voice their protest. (pp. 65–66)

6

The Apostles' Testimony

In chapter 4 I observed that during his own ministry Jesus sent his disciples out to proclaim his message. After the crucifixion, the "apostles" did not stop doing so. They carried on, but under different circumstances. (p. 38)

The shocking events around the Passover in Jerusalem had changed everything. According to the beginning of the book of Acts, for Jesus' disciples there was initially a time of silence and waiting. At the festival of Pentecost that followed, they were "filled with the Holy Spirit" and began to proclaim his message in a new manner. (Acts 2)

Everything was now new—and yet it was a continuation of what Jesus had begun. Alhough it might appear otherwise, the mission of the disciples was not essentially different from that of their master. We have come to recognize that Jesus' gospel was a reform movement within Judaism.

Witnesses to the Crucified Messiah

For the disciples, the fundamental difference between past and present was that Jesus was no longer with them. He had been condemned by the Sanhedrin and executed by the Romans. This had a clear effect.

The proclamation of his gospel was henceforth accompanied by a protest against his unjust execution. The witness of Jesus' disciples originally had also a juridical significance: it was testimony for Jesus.

In this an important statement concerning the meaning of *the cross* is made. One of the original interpretations was that it was an unjust and ignominious death—a curse, says Paul—that Jesus did not deserve. This was how many Jews who were not among his followers saw it, including not a few Pharisees; it was even more the case that his followers viewed the matter in this way. (Galatians 3:13; p. 55)

But it is clear that Jesus' followers also ascribed a theological significance to his crucifixion. In this they probably linked up with certain allusions made by Jesus himself. I have mentioned the importance of the figure of Isaac, the "beloved son" who must die. In doing so, the disciples did not deny that the cross was also an injustice. Both aspects are expressed in the following saying: "The Son of Man goes as it is written of him, *but woe to that one by whom* the Son of Man is betrayed!" (Mark 14:21; pp. 47, 48)

In their testimony Jesus' disciples did not hesitate to identify the guilty party. We gather this from several speeches recorded in the Acts of the Apostles. Along with the Gospel of Luke, Acts was written toward the end of the first century. The writer gives a quite balanced depiction of the Jews and makes respectful use of older traditions. In the speeches contained in Acts, the author's hand is clearly recognizable, but here too he uses older elements.

According to these speeches, Jesus' disciples viewed the cross as an injustice that involved all of Israel. This is understandable. An occurrence such as a murder makes an appeal to the onlookers. Whoever stands idly by is indirectly implicated. Thus Peter said to the people of Jerusalem, "Jesus of Nazareth . . . you crucified and killed by the hands of those outside the law. But God raised him up," and, "You killed the Author of life, whom God raised from the dead." The rare designation of Jesus as "Author of life" does not appear to have been thought up by the writer, and the same must be true of the characterization of the Romans as "those outside the law." In the same breath the resurrection is also mentioned (to which I shall return). In his speech to the centurion from Caesarea who sympathized with Judaism, Peter summarized as follows, "We are witnesses to all that he did both in Judea and in Jerusalem. They put him to death by hanging him on a tree; but God raised him on the third day. . . ." (Acts 2:22; 3:15; 10:39)

That the author of Acts here made use of ancient traditions is apparent as well from a motif in Stephen's speech. When summoned to appear before the Sanhedrin, Stephen addressed the high priest and the others present, "Which of the prophets did your ancestors not persecute? They killed those who foretold the coming of the Righteous One, and now you have become his betrayers and murderers." This motif of the murder of the prophets was a widespread theme in ancient Jewish literature. Legend has it that Isaiah and Jeremiah were also killed by the people. Reference to this motif is also ascribed to Jesus: "Jerusalem, Jerusalem, the city that kills the prophets and stones those who are sent to it!" The motif played a key role in the earliest beginnings of Christianity. Not only was Stephen killed but so also his master and his master's teacher, John the Baptist. (Acts 7:52; Luke 13:34)

The accusation that accompanied the testimony of the cross was thus not an exception. According to Jesus' disciples, his death was one of a series of murders of prophets. The speeches in Acts declare Jesus not only to be the crucified one. In the first place, they proclaim that he was "the Holy and Righteous One," "a man attested to you by God," one "anointed . . . with the Holy Spirit and with power." These, too, are probably ancient motifs. Jesus was thus viewed of old as a prophetic, even messianic figure. His own hopeful message of the imminent kingdom of God for the poor is hereby brought to mind, his gospel in which he also involved his disciples and in which he himself played a central role. His crucifixion was thus so much the more an injustice. (Acts 3:14; 2:22; 10:38)

The witness of the apostles concerning the crucifixion did not imply an anti-Jewish standpoint. It was an *intra-Jewish* protest, in which the disciples, following the example of the prophets, accused the people of their transgressions. This is how John the Baptist and Jesus had acted as well with their summons to repent in view of the nearness of God's kingdom. Later, when followers of Jesus started using this testimony against the Jews as a whole, things were to change. It then became a charge to reject the Jews, no longer a summons to repentance from within the Jewish context.

After the memorable festival of Pentecost, Jesus' disciples began openly to proclaim him as the Messiah. It is possible that the crucifixion itself gave impetus to this. One of the least controversial facts about Jesus is the inscription Pilate had put on the cross—according to John in three languages—"King of the Jews." The reports do not say that Jesus had claimed this title in so many words nor that his disciples had claimed it for him. The allegation was rather incorporated into the accusation of the chief priests. In any case, it is not improbable that once it was thus published, the disciples adopted it. "King of the Jews" was simply the Roman and political translation of what the Jews called "Messiah"—the Anointed One or, in Greek, "the Christ." (Mark 15:26; John 19:19; p. 47)

Jesus' descent from King David could have played a role in this. Along with the elements mentioned above, we find this motif at the end of Peter's first speech to the people of Jerusalem in Acts. He quotes a psalm traditionally ascribed to David: "'David did not ascend into the heavens, but he himself says, "The Lord said to my Lord, 'Sit at my right hand. . . .'"' Therefore let the entire house of Israel know with certainty that God has made him both Lord and Messiah, this Jesus whom you have crucified." (Acts 2:34; Ps 110:1; p. 34)

Thus the crucifixion did not bring the Jesus movement to an end. On the contrary, the decision of the Jerusalem chief priests to execute the preacher from Nazareth only made the discussion about his significance more heated. His followers were the more convinced of his key role in the history of Israel.

"Who Was Raised on the Third Day"

The new proclamation of the gospel after Pentecost carried with it a renewed understanding of the writings of Moses and the prophets. We have seen that Jesus' gospel, too, was based on intensive study of these ancient writings, just as was the message of his former teacher, John. Jesus' disciples pursued this further in the altered situation. A central element of their testimony was related directly to this: the resurrection of Jesus, or his rising from the dead. (p. 36)

Exactly what happened on Sunday morning in that Passover week we shall never know. According to Matthew, to refute the report of his resurrection, the chief priests and Pharisees spread the rumor that Jesus' disciples had removed his body. Within the circle of his disciples itself, the report was passed on that the grave was found empty, first by several women, later by a couple of disciples. These reports are confused and fragmentary. (Matthew 27:62; Mark 16:1; Luke 24:1; John 20:1)

Every consideration of this much-discussed event is pointless as long as it is viewed as an isolated physical phenomenon. In a literal sense, the "resurrection from the dead" is "inconceivable." That is, whatever this concept signifies transcends not only the limitations of the human body but also all human understanding. It can only be meaningful in a broader context. And that is precisely how we encounter it. We have seen that the testimony of Jesus' disciples concerning his resurrection is mentioned in the same breath as the injustice of his crucifixion. Moreover, affirming Jesus' resurrection has no significance isolated from the general belief in the raising of the dead at the end of time. Finally, the apostolic testimony that he was raised "on the third day" is understandable only in relation to the prophetic writings.

In the Old Testament, the belief in the resurrection at the end of time occurs hardly at all. It must have originated among the Jews during or after the Babylonian exile, possibly due to the influence of related ideas of the Persian rulers. Only after the beginning of the Persian period is the revival of the dead at the end of time spoken of—for example, in the latest book of the Old Testament, Daniel: "Many of those who sleep in the dust of the earth shall awake, some to everlasting life, and some to shame and everlasting contempt." In a late text in Isaiah there are these enigmatic words: "Your dead shall live, their corpses shall rise. O dwellers in the dust, awake and sing for joy!" We find the belief in the resurrection also in later Jewish texts. One idea is that martyrs shall rise to share in well-earned glory, but their executioners shall awake to judgment. (Daniel 12:2; Isaiah 26:19)

In the older portions of the Old Testament, such as the five "books of Moses," the Pentateuch, resurrection is not mentioned. In Jesus' time the issue was controversial. The Sadducees rejected the belief in the resurrection because it was not found in the books of Moses. In this they differed with most others, notably the Pharisees. The latter adduced all possible details in the Bible to "prove" the resurrection. Typical is the report in the Gospels in which the Sadducees confront Jesus with a regulation from the law of Moses that would seem to reduce the idea of resurrection to an absurdity. Jesus answered, however, that they knew "neither the Scriptures nor the power of God." As proof he cited a text in which God revealed himself to Moses as "the God of Abraham, the God of Isaac, and the God of Jacob." His conclusion was that "He is God not of the dead, but of the living." Objectively considered, the argumentation is rather far-fetched, but the same kind of creative interpretation can be found in the scriptural "proofs" of the Pharisees. (Mark 12:18; Exodus 3:6; p. 65)

Along with his disciples, Jesus belonged to the majority of Jews who believed that at the end of time God would revive the righteous to eternal life. This was an essential part of the coming kingdom of God. The fact that the apostles declared that Jesus had been raised from the dead means that they believed that in him this future had already begun. In the metaphors Paul used, Jesus is thus called "the *firstborn* from the dead," "the *first fruits* of those who have died." Thus viewed, his resurrection is "an advance on the future" that is reserved for all believers. (Colossians 1:18; 1 Corinthians 15:20)

Here too it is possible that Jesus himself gave rise to his disciples' belief. Included in his words during the last supper is the statement, "I have eagerly desired to eat this Passover with you . . . for I tell you that from now on I will not drink of the fruit of the vine until the kingdom of God comes." The intention is not fully clear, but, whatever was meant, at that moment Jesus spoke about his share in the coming kingdom of God and thus in the resurrection of the dead. (Luke 22:15; p. 47)

In any event, it is true that his disciples subsequently understood it in this manner. It is acknowledged in so many words in various places to be a retrospective understanding. These texts therefore contain some of the most trustworthy information in the Gospels. The Gospel of John is particularly candid. When Jesus' disciples discovered an empty tomb, they did not at first know what had happened, "for as yet they did not understand the scripture, that he must rise from the dead." The same is said with reference to Jesus' enigmatic statement concerning the "destroying" and "rebuilding" of the temple: "After he was raised from the dead, his disciples remembered that he had said this, and they believed the scripture and the word that Jesus had spoken." (John 2:22; 20:9; 14:26)

With consummate skill the same is expressed in a story in Luke. Two disciples were on their way in the evening from Jerusalem to their village of Emmaus. They had been told that Jesus was resurrected, but they could not comprehend that. They expressed their disappointment about Jesus' sad fate to a third one who had joined them: "We had hoped that he was the one to redeem Israel. Yes, and besides all this, it is now the third day since these things took place." Nor did they understand it at all when the stranger proceeded to explain the happenings from "Moses and all the prophets." Upon arriving at their village, they invited him to eat and asked him to open the meal. He took the bread, pronounced the blessing, and broke it. At that moment "their eyes were opened, and they recognized him." Only then did they understand all those verses Jesus had explained along the way—for it was he. They returned to Jerusalem and related to the other disciples "how he had been made known to them in the breaking of the bread." (Luke 24:13)

A key expression in this story is "the third day." It occurs in many other passages concerning Jesus' resurrection, for example, in the announcement he himself makes: "The Son of Man must undergo great suffering, and be rejected by the elders, chief priests, and scribes, and be killed, and *on the third day* be raised." Other passages have the form of a creed. Paul cites one of them: "I handed on to you as of first importance what I in turn had received: that Christ died for our sins in accordance with the scriptures, and that he was buried, and that he was raised *on the third day* in accordance with the scriptures." (Luke 9:22; 1 Corinthians 15:3)

Here again the motif of the third day is marked by the disciples' retrospective understanding, although it cannot be excluded that Jesus had already alluded to it. We read at the end of Luke that the Resurrected One appeared to his disciples and "opened their minds *to understand the scriptures* . . . that the Messiah is to suffer and to rise from the dead on the third day." This seems to refer to a biblical text. Paul explicitly makes such a reference: "on the third day in *accordance with the scriptures*." The intended verse must be the one from Hosea: "After two days he will revive us; *on the third day he will raise* us up, that we may live before him." (Luke 24:45; 1 Corinthians 15:3; Hosea 6:2)

In the light of the Scriptures freshly read, Jesus' disciples testified concerning his momentous final days in Jerusalem. Many texts and motifs converge in this. Jesus is confessed to be the Anointed One, the Beloved Son who died on a cross, who arose from the dead on the third day, and who is seated at the right hand of God, from which he, the Son of Man, shall come to pronounce judgment, and whose kingdom shall know no end." All these elements are to be found in the Judaism of that time, and they were nurtured by an intense rereading of the Old Testament. Thus the apostles summarized the pivotal significance Jesus had in the history of Israel. In theological terms: *the most ancient Christology* is composed of elements that Jesus' Jewish disciples read associatively from the Old Testament. Later creeds further elaborated this.

For his followers, therefore, Jesus' dying on the cross was not in vain. They saw it in the light of his own message of hope about God's kingdom that would soon come. With renewed energy, they propagated this "gospel," first among the Jews and later also among the non-Jews.

"Jewish Churches" under Peter and James

Jesus' disciples not only traveled about; they also met together regularly. According to the book of Acts there was a community in Jerusalem in which they read the Scriptures, said prayers, and "broke bread" in Jesus' name. As with the two on the road to Emmaus, the memory of the meals they had shared with Jesus was kept alive. Besides this, they continued to participate in temple worship. According to reports in Mark and Matthew, churches must also have arisen in Galilee. That is where the disciples had "seen" their risen master. Thus in various places in the Jewish homeland, communities of Jesus' followers emerged. These were, so to speak, "Jewish churches." (Acts 2:42; Mark 16:7; Matthew 28:16)

The words "church" and "Jewish" are here not used in the usual manner. It is conventional to contrast Christianity with Judaism, church with synagogue. This fits the contemporary situation. But in the beginning it was not so. The first churches comprised Jews who were indistinguishable from their fellow Jews in everything except in the significance they ascribed to Jesus. They circumcised their sons, followed the dietary regulations, celebrated the Jewish festivals and especially the Sabbath, and took part in the worship in the synagogue and the temple. Along with this they met to proclaim and celebrate that Jesus was the promised Messiah. That is why they were "Jewish churches." Their Jewish belief in Jesus was the basis of all later Christianity.

Although not customary, the word "church" is appropriate here. In origin, it is not a "Christian" word. It is related to the Greek word *ekklesia* from the Greek translation of the Old Testament, and is the designation for the solemn "assembly" that Moses regularly convened. The other Greek term for this also became well known: *synagogue*. Both words mean simply "meeting." Church and synagogue are thus at least linguistically related. The Jewish-Christian background of the word "church" is intimated when Paul speaks of "the churches of God . . . in Judea." Comparable expressions were used in Qumran. (1 Thessalonians 2:14)

The Jewish churches differed from the various synagogues actually only in their view of Jesus, that is, in their *Christology*. This involved a particular view of the significance of Jesus within the framework of the Bible and of Israel's history. The tradition of his own teachings also played an important role. In other respects, these churches were not fundamentally distinguishable from other Jewish congregations. For this reason later church fathers, obviously non-Jewish, accused Jewish Christians of observing the purity laws and circumcision.

That Jewish churches arose quite early in Galilee is not surprising. According to Mark and John, Jesus himself came from there, as did his most prominent disciples. Luke and Acts give the impression that the church in Jerusalem was more eminent, which indeed could have been the case at times.

According to various reports, the Jerusalem church was originally under the leadership of Jesus' most prominent disciple, Peter—himself also a Galilean. His name was actually Simon, but Jesus, as teachers were accustomed to do, gave him a disciple's name, "Rock." In Aramaic this is *Kifa*, a name that occurs in the New Testament more often than "Peter." Paul customarily employs the Greek form of this, *Kefas* (NRSV: Cephas). The later sources, the Gospels and Acts, use the translated form "Peter," from the Greek *petra*, "rock." (Mark 3:16; John 1:42; Acts 10:18)

Matthew makes the importance of Peter clear: Jesus gave him this name because, he said, "on this rock I will build my church." This phrase reflects the perspective of Matthew's church. But Paul also spoke of Peter's importance. Paul related how, long after his conversion, he returned to Jerusalem. He stayed two weeks with Cephas and, of the other apostles, visited only with James. According to a tradition Paul cited elsewhere, after his resurrection, Jesus appeared first to Peter of all the apostles. Furthermore, at the beginning of Acts, Peter is said to have acted as the primary spokesman of the church. He, too, visited the churches in the diaspora. Paul noted that Peter had been in Corinth; a later tradition puts him also in Rome. (Matthew 16:18; Galatians 1:18; Acts 2:14; 1 Corinthians 9:5; 15:5)

After Peter, James became prominent in the Jerusalem church. The oldest testimony comes from Paul, who called him "the Lord's brother," referring to him as one of the leaders of the church in Jerusalem. According to an account in Mark, he was Jesus' oldest brother, thus the second son of Mary. Jesus' brothers must at first have been skeptical of his message, but they apparently joined the church quite early. According to the tradition Paul hands on, the Risen One finally also appeared to James. Half way through the book of Acts, James appears to have assumed the leadership of the church in Jerusalem. In later traditions he counts as the first bishop of Jerusalem. Jewish Christians always held him in high esteem. (Mark 6:3; Galatians 1:19; 1 Corinthians 15:7; Acts 15:13)

Little is known of the churches in the region of Galilee. Toward the end of the first century we again hear of them. According to a report of the church fathers, the Roman emperor of that time, Domitian, was apprehensive of messianic movements among the Jews. But when he had Jesus' family members questioned, they appeared to be simple Galilean peasants, and he released them with disdain. This account seems to indicate that Jesus' family was held in high regard in the churches in the Jewish homeland. Perhaps this contributed to the fact that James became the leader of the Jerusalem church.

The New Testament contains two letters that could have originated in the churches in the Jewish homeland. The authors present themselves as "James" and "Jude . . . brother of James," apparently indicating the brothers of Jesus. James emphasizes keeping the law and even in one place designates the church as "synagogue" (2:2; the NRSV translates "assembly"). (p. 118)

It must have been in the churches in the Jewish homeland that the tradition of Jesus' words was first preserved. I have referred to this oral tradition and to the written Gospels that issued from it. I concluded that Jesus' teachings are preserved in the purest form in Mark, Luke, and Matthew. Moreover, we saw that in these texts Peter, the leader of the Jerusalem church, played the main role. It is clear that these three Gospels are our earliest and most important sources for the tradition of Jesus' disciples, the *apostolic tradition*. Nonetheless, the Fourth Gospel also contains essential information concerning Jesus and his first disciples. (p. 19)

In the course of history, the Jewish churches were persecuted and eventually disappeared entirely. Little else of their writings is preserved. This came about because the dominant form of Christianity became detached and wholly alienated from its Jewish roots, a development that can be traced even in most of the Gospels.

Paul's Churches of Non-Jews

The cause of church's detachment from its Jewish roots is usually ascribed to Paul. He is said to have abolished the Jewish law in practice. A growing number of scholars now find this untenable. According to them, Paul's vehement protests are not directed against the law itself but against making the law binding on non-Jewish Christians. The issue played a role in the network of churches that Paul and his co-workers founded in Syria, Asia Minor, Greece, and Italy. Paul's own letters and the book of Acts tell us of this.

The most explicit source on this issue is Paul's protest in his letter to the church in Galatia, the region surrounding present-day Ankara. Paul himself had founded that church, but other preachers had come there and contended that believing non-Jews must be circumcised. According to Paul, they sought hereby to avoid being "persecuted for the cross of Christ." Apparently, some Jewish Christians were suspicious of non-Jewish Christians. This was around the middle of the first century, when the atmosphere between Jews and non-Jews generally became more tense and culminated in the Jewish war with Rome. Most of Paul's letters were written during the 50s and attest to this tension. (Galatians 6:12)

There are, however, also letters of Paul in which this tension does not come to the fore. Among these is 1 Corinthians, which dates from the same period. Within the Pauline churches the relation between Jews and non-Jews was not always and everywhere problematic. It is the more remarkable that 2 Corinthians, written one or two years after the first, does give evidence of such tension. In the intervening period, the situation with respect to the issue of the Jewish law must have worsened in Corinth as well.

It seems that the tide turned against Paul during the 50s. Gradually the notion gained ground among Jewish Christians that non-Jews were not full-fledged Christians unless they became Jewish. Paul resisted this with all he had, but he could not turn the tide. Non-Jewish Christians reacted as well. We know of this from the church in Rome. In Paul's letter to the Roman Christians, he comments on the irritation of non-Jewish Christians with the Jewish lifestyle. This was a rather basic and direct anti-Jewish reaction, which did not, of course, simplify Paul's position within the Jewish world. He found himself forced to defend himself against the charge that he encouraged Jewish Christians to turn away from the law. It is also for this reason that he eventually was arrested in Jerusalem. (Galatians 2:11; Romans 11:13; 9:3; 3:8; Acts 21:21)

In the beginning it must have been different. In the letter to Galatia, Paul reports an agreement he had made with the apostles in Jerusalem several years previously. They acknowledged his work among non-Jews, while he accepted their responsibility for Jewish Christians. This entailed mutual respect. Jewish Christians were to respect the lifestyle of non-Jewish Christians, and vice versa. (Galatians 2:9)

In another letter, Paul expresses precisely this matter in a rule that he says he prescribed *to all churches*: "Was anyone at the time of his call already circumcised? Let him not seek to remove the marks of circumcision. Was anyone at the time of his call uncircumcised? Let him not seek circumcision." In the past, circumcision had been undone by Jews who wanted to participate in Greek sports, in which the athletes were naked; many Greeks considered circumcision to be disfiguration. Paul argues that the one who as a Jew is called to faith in Jesus should continue living as a Jew, but the non-Jew who comes to believe should not become Jewish. (1 Corinthians 7:17)

Paul mentions the rule three times in his letter to the Galatians. This is striking because in Galatians he fulminates against the pressure on non-Jewish Christians to become Jews. The first half of the rule—that the circumcised Christian should continue to live as a Jew—has nothing to do with the issue at hand. A basic rule is being cited. As stated by Paul, the rule accords with the apostolic agreement that he mentioned earlier in the letter. (Galatians 3:28; 5:6; 6:15)

Several more general facts confirm this interpretation. There are clear indications that Paul respected the apostolic tradition honored by the churches of the Jewish homeland. He also speaks positively about Cephas and Jesus' brother James, the first leaders of the church in Jerusalem. Furthermore, the collection of money he organized for the poor of the Jerusalem church is significant. He wrote several times about this as a proof of his positive attitude toward the Jewish churches. (1 Corinthians 11:23; 9:5; 16:4; Galatians 1:18; 2:10)

In an announcement to Jewish fellow Christians, Paul in one place calls "his" churches "churches of the Gentiles." Although there were also Jewish members, these churches had mainly non-Jewish membership. Paul's rule meant that they must respect the lifestyle of their Jewish fellow believers, for "circumcision is nothing, and uncircumcision is nothing." On the other hand, Jewish Christians were not to despise their non-Jewish brothers and sisters. This was all in line with the apostolic agreement in Jerusalem, which called for mutual respect between Jewish and non-Jewish Christians. (Romans 16:4; 1 Corinthians 7:19)

The descriptions in Acts confirm this interpretation of Paul. We are told that he was born in Tarsus of Cilicia, but raised in Jerusalem as a Pharisee. He had studied "at the feet of Gamaliel," the popular and respected Pharisee leader. At first Paul was a fierce opponent of Jesus' disciples, but when he had a vision of the one whom he persecuted, everything changed. He recognized Jesus as Messiah and dedicated himself to preaching to non-Jews. That did not mean that he left Judaism. Paul remained faithful to his people and to the law. (Acts 22:3; 5:34; 9:3; 21:26; 28:17; p. 61)

Acts also mentions the apostolic agreement. Also according to this report it was agreed that the non-Jewish Christians did not have to become Jewish. They were obliged to observe certain general regulations, such as the prohibition of idolatry and illicit sexual relations. Paul does not explicitly mention such requisites, but he does use strongly related rules in his instructions to the non-Jewish Christians in Corinth. We can therefore speak of a general concord between the two accounts. (Acts 15:6; 1 Corinthians 5:1; 8:1; 12:2)

Paul did not operate alone. In his letters, many co-workers are mentioned, both Jews and non-Jews. His younger colleagues, Timothy and Titus, are well known. And Peter and others had preceded him in the proclamation of Jesus' gospel in the world. The church in Rome was founded prior to Paul, but he felt a close tie to it. In his letter to Rome, he announced his intention to travel to Spain. An ancient tradition says that he did just that. According to this tradition, he later returned to Rome and there, just like Peter, died as a martyr. There are various indications that Peter was held in high esteem not only in Rome but in all of Paul's churches. The book of Acts places the two apostles side by side as the two mainstays of the one church comprising Jews and non-Jews. (Romans 15:28)

Johannine Churches and Other Christians

Our information about the earliest churches is sparse. Thus far I have discussed only the best-known ones, those that are the focus of our major sources, the network of Pauline churches in Asia Minor and Greece and the churches in the Jewish homeland. Besides these, there are significant traces of other groups.

The Gospel of John gives evidence of such. John has its own distinctive language as well as a distinctive view of Jesus' words and deeds. It reflects a community with a rather closed view of the world and of itself. Moreover, there is a striking difference in the position accorded to Peter. The most prominent disciple is an unnamed individual who at the last supper reclined at Jesus' right, the place of highest honor. This disciple appears to be closer to Jesus than Peter was. This seems to reflect a faction that was completely separate from the churches to which the other three Gospels belonged. (John 13:23)

The epistles of John strongly resemble the Gospel in language and atmosphere; they must derive from the same tradition. Here, however, we get the impression of diverse churches with tensions among them. Together, therefore, the Johannine churches must for some time have led their own separate existence alongside the churches in which Peter and Paul were honored. Later the distance appears to have lessened. In the second century, the Gospel of John was adopted by the "apostolic" churches, first in Asia Minor. The church in Rome still had doubts about it.

In the meantime there were other developments. From the middle of the second century, we have reports of various groups and teachers who were opposed by the apostolic churches. In Rome, *Marcion* attracted attention by sharply contrasting the Old Testament with Jesus. In fact, he did not recognize the Old Testament as scripture. Related to him were the adherents of *Gnosticism*, a term that means "teachings of knowledge." These groups, too, had little appreciation for the Old Testament. They ascribed creation to a deity other than the Father of Jesus and emphasized the misery of humanity in the vale of tears of this earthly existence. Salvation, according to them, comes only through secret "knowledge" (*gnosis*) revealed from a heavenly source.

These factions and sects are difficult to chart, because their various teachers and groups continuously contradict each other. They emerged during the second century but must have had their roots in the first century. Possibly—especially in Egypt and Syria—they were far more numerous than our traditional sources admit. In all events they give testimony to the multiform character of earliest Christianity.

In contrast, the churches of Paul and Peter emphatically held to the Old Testament. The church of Rome excommunicated Marcion in 144 C.E. and sharply opposed the Gnostic teachers. During this time, the churches that later came to be considered "orthodox" were perhaps a minority. They began to call themselves *apostolic*, after the tradition to which they adhered. Nonetheless, a fundamental difference with the original testimony of the apostles had arisen: the apostolic churches of the second century had become detached from their Jewish foundations. And that lay behind their resistance to Jewish Christians.

7

The Impact of
the War with Rome

In previous chapters I have mentioned the great war of the Jews with Rome in 66–70 C.E. This traumatic historical event now deserves separate attention. It was accompanied by sweeping social changes and became a turning point in the relationships among Jews themselves—and between Christians and Jews.

Jews and Non-Jews in Antioch

The changes occasioned by the war can be observed in the city of Antioch, present-day Antakya in the southeastern corner of Turkey, at the bend of the coast close to Syria. During the Hellenistic period Antioch was the capital of the Graeco-Syrian kingdom. Also in the Roman period it was a government and trade center, situated at a crossroads of the roads going south to the Jewish homeland and Egypt and those going east to Babylonia, Persia, and India. Its large Jewish community lived in an open relationship with fellow citizens. Josephus relates that many non-Jews customarily came to the synagogue services. Antiochian church leaders would later take a sharply anti-Jewish position, apparently in an attempt to counter the continuing interest of their parishioners in the synagogue.

According to two of our New Testament sources, the first important church outside of the Jewish homeland was in Antioch. Paul wrote about it as consisting of many Jews and non-Jews. Apostles from Jerusalem visited regularly, and Jews shared meals with non-Jews. Acts relates that Paul and his companion Barnabas lived and taught there for a year and a half. Members of the church were first called "Christians" there. This term apparently designated both Jewish and non-Jewish believers. Antioch was all of this—crossroads, meeting point between east and west, birthplace of the first "Christian" church—and the first church of which we know with certainty that Jews and non-Jews came to oppose one another. (Galatians 2:11; Acts 11:26; 15:1)

Both Paul and Acts report conflict in Antioch, but these reports do not agree. The simplest explanation appears to be that two different conflicts are reported. Acts tells of a quarrel in Antioch about requiring circumcision and other commandments of non-Jewish Christians. Paul and Barnabas were sent to Jerusalem. The agreement of the apostles (discussed above) ensued. This must have been at the end of the 40s. Paul, too, reports a clash, but at some point *after* the agreement. This time it was not about commandments for the non-Jews themselves but about sharing meals with Jewish Christians. Up to that point, Jews and non-Jews ate together in the church. However, "certain people came from James," and the Jews began to eat separately, "even Barnabas." They no longer wanted to appear connected to Christians of Gentile background. With this, the apostolic agreement faltered. Paul came to stand alone, opposite most other Jewish Christians. His letter to Rome, written somewhat later, also reflects this development. He writes there that he was traveling with a collection for the church in Jerusalem. He was not certain that this would be appreciated. He was apprehensive of "the unbelievers in Judea." (Acts 15:1; Galatians 2:11; Romans 15:31; p. 88)

These two conflicts must be viewed within the context of a broader development. From other sources we know that at the end of the 50s, tensions between Jews and non-Jews had mounted not only in Judea but also in Antioch. Josephus reports violent outbursts at the beginning of the war. This is striking, because he also tells of open relationships in the city. Apparently, the social climate had gravely deteriorated. It is thus plausible that the difficulties Paul faced were not merely resistance to his gospel.

The Jews in the Antioch church had previously been accustomed to sharing meals with him and with non-Jews. But now they, too, had come to
resent association with non-Jews. It appears that a more general aversion
toward non-Jews grew among the Jews. Opposition to Roman domination would have played a prominent role in this.

These things could not have left the non-Jewish Christians unaf-
fected. We have noticed traces of an anti-Jewish reaction in Paul's letter
to Rome. What he feared there actually took place in Antioch. After the
war, a separate non-Jewish church emerged, as can be observed in the letters of Ignatius, the bishop of Antioch at the end of the first century. In
a biting tone he warned that the followers of Jesus may not keep Jewish
commandments such as the Sabbath. He explicitly placed Christianity
in opposition to Judaism. He viewed Judaism as a dangerous competi-
tor, because many of his parishioners felt attracted to it. The result of
this attitude was an anti-Jewish Christianity. What the bishop articulated
was not an individual point of view. Thus Antioch became the first place
where *anti-Judaism* was documented, that is, a reaction against Judaism as
such. (p. 88)

It did not stop at this. At the end of the fourth century the church in
Antioch had an eloquent dean, John, surnamed Chrysostom or "Golden
Mouth." Eight of his sermons against the Jews have been preserved. In
these he denigrates Judaism in the unrefined manner customary at that
time. He evidently had reason for this: there must still have been Antio-
chian Gentiles in the church who were drawn toward synagogue services.
Nonetheless, in spite of the sympathy of the people, the anti-Judaism of
Ignatius had by then set the tone in the non-Jewish church.

It is possible, nevertheless, to say something more positive about
Antioch. In Luke and Acts, a totally different, more open relationship
with the Jews is presented. According to church tradition, the author himself hailed from Antioch. If this be true, at the end of the first century in
that city there were still those who remained faithful to Paul's ideal of one
church comprising Jews and non-Jews. (p. 111)

Lovers of War and Lovers of Peace

Both in Antioch and elsewhere, the tensions between Jewish and non-
Jewish Christians were related to the Jewish war with Rome. This raises
the question about the responsibility for the war, a question as old as the

war itself. In many respects it appeared to be a civil war. Josephus, our most important source of information, gives ample attention to it.

As with all historiographers, in his report Josephus aimed at defending certain interests. He defended not only his own interests and those of his imperial patrons but also those of his own people. His account generally suggests that the Jews as a whole were not to blame for the war and the disasters that came from it. He places the fault with radical groups that had drawn the people into the revolt. According to him, one of those groups included Pharisees, with this difference: they gave top priority to political freedom. Many other Pharisees were not sympathetic to the revolt. Here we must recall that Josephus elsewhere informs his readers that he himself belonged to the Pharisees. He thus defended the Pharisees as well, in particular against the accusation that they too were responsible for the war. (p. 30)

The lack of unity among the Pharisees concerning the war is confirmed by rabbinic literature. According to tradition, Yohanan ben Zakkai let himself be smuggled out of Jerusalem in a coffin during the siege of the city. A leading Pharisee from the school of Hillel, he opposed the war. This comes out also in his critical statements about war in general. Other representatives of that school also voiced their criticism of the war. In contrast, the adherents of the school of Shammai were squarely behind the revolt. They did not even shrink from using violence against peaceable fellow Pharisees. The conflict in which the Shammaites enforced anti-Gentile regulations upon the Hillelites has been mentioned. Along with other facts, this leads to the conclusion that the Pharisaic school of Shammai was closely connected to the radicals about whom Josephus wrote. (p. 32)

This conclusion is highly significant for early Christian history. It confirms the suspicion that the discord among Jewish Christians concerning the attitude toward non-Jews should be viewed within a broader context. During the period before the war, many Jewish Christians no longer wanted to appear to be connected to Gentile believers. These Jewish Christians also were apparently influenced by the radical climate that was evident in the school of Shammai.

In Paul's day the tensions were still merely between different points of view. The war set everything on edge and confronted Jewish and non-Jewish Christians with an acute dilemma. Were they to choose in favor of the war-inclined Jews and thus keep their distance from their non-Jewish brothers and sisters? Or were they to opt for the peace-loving party and break with the radical Jewish Christians? One thing was certain. In this climate the relationships between Jews and non-Jews in the churches could only deteriorate.

Rabbinic Judaism

Jewish society itself was changed drastically by the war with Rome. Two influential groups disappeared entirely. After the war, nothing more was heard of the Essenes. From excavations it has become apparent that their center near the Dead Sea was destroyed by the Romans. The Sadducees disappeared from stage as well. Along with the temple, their position of power was destroyed. The Pharisees were the only significant group that remained. Leadership of the people fell to them.

Within the Pharisaic movement itself, however, an important shift had taken place. The school of Shammai was now greatly in the minority. In the mounting climate of war, they must have been even more popular than the Hillelites just prior to the war. The subsequent shift must in any event be related to the course of the war. The Shammaites were more bellicose than the Hillelites, their involvement in the strife was greater, and thus they must have suffered more casualties. All this changed the nature of Judaism.

A basic attitude of the Hillelites was to tolerate differences of opinion and to consider the opinions cherished by the people. This disposition is related of Hillel himself. Once there was disagreement about whether the Passover sacrifice could be slaughtered on a Sabbath. When Hillel was consulted, he appealed to scriptural arguments according to which the festival sacrifice is more important than the Sabbath. But Hillel considered determinative what the people were accustomed to. What turned out to be the case? All along the people had been following the opinion advocated by Hillel! Another significant example has to do with the anti-Gentile measures that the Shammaites had enforced. The Talmud reports that a number of these later fell into disuse among the people. The tradition of Hillel is mentioned in this regard, and the saying is cited, "One must not issue a rule that the majority of the community cannot keep."

The postwar situation brought a crisis of leadership. The Jewish community was left adrift by the fall of the temple and of the administrative bodies connected to it, such as the highest court of justice. The political position of the Jews within the Roman empire was now weakened as well. Various measures dating from this period indicate a tendency toward internal consolidation. The relationship with Christians was also affected. Among other innovations, a main prayer of the synagogue liturgy was introduced in which an existing prayer against "heretics and renegades" was altered to target Jewish Christians. The effect was that the latter could not join the prayers in the synagogue. This measure, however, was apparently not applied everywhere and to an equal degree.

Another measure was the establishment of the officially recognized teacher of the law—*rabbi*, literally, "my master." Previously this was used as a polite form of address, not as a formalized title. Jesus, too, was thus addressed. In spite of his importance, Hillel is not referred to as "Rabbi Hillel." Teachers after the war, however, were designated as "Rabbi Akiba," etc. (Mark 9:5; John 1:38)

Therefore, from this point on we speak of rabbis and of *rabbinic Judaism*. It can be seen as a continuation of the Pharisaic tradition, the most important difference being that the tradition of Hillel then became dominant. Rabbinic literature began to emerge as well, its best known writings being the *Talmud* and the *Midrashim*. (p. 31)

In a certain sense, then, rabbinic Judaism is a product of the war with Rome. The opposition to Christianity can be easily understood in the postwar climate. It corresponds to the *anti-Jewish* attitude that developed at the same time within the non-Jewish churches. On both sides positions hardened. Nonetheless, in this period we still hear of an encounter between a rabbi and a follower of Jesus, in which the renowned Rabbi Eliezer heard from some Galilean a tradition handed down from Jesus that pleased him. It led to difficulties for him, for the Roman authorities suspected him of sympathizing with Christianity. This detail brings to mind Roman measures against Christians in Asia Minor toward the end of the first century, of which we know from a letter of the local governor, Pliny the Younger.

From 132 to 135 the second great revolt against Rome raged in the Jewish homeland. It was led by Simon bar Kokhba. According to the influential Rabbi Akiba, bar Kokhba was the Messiah, but another rabbi thought this to be a fallacy. Bar Kokhba's revolt resulted in many victims among his own ranks. There are reports that these included Jewish Christians. Even apart from all the casualties, this war had more far-reaching effects than the first one. Judea was thoroughly razed. Jews were no longer allowed to live in Jerusalem, where a temple for Jupiter was established. Nonetheless, at the end of the second and beginning of the third century, Judaism flourished in Galilee. The most important rabbinic writings were completed at that time. The great decline in the Jewish homeland came only in the fourth century under the Christian emperor Constantine.

The Emergence of an Anti-Jewish Theology

Already before the war of 66–70, social divisions increased. We have seen how Paul had to contend with tensions between Jews and non-Jews within his churches. Clashes, some quite fierce, of Jewish Christians with synagogues also occurred. Paul mentions that five times he had been given the "forty lashes minus one," the punishment that synagogues could impose on rebels. The war must have aggravated the situation. In various places the result was a complete break. (2 Corinthians 11:24)

The war and its aftermath had the effect of bringing uniformity to the various Jewish and Christian communities. Judaism previously was composed of multiple movements and schools. After the war there was much less diversity. Sadducees and Essenes disappeared, the Shammaites came to be a small minority, the Hillelites became dominant, and Jewish Christians were often no longer tolerated. Before the war, the followers of Jesus also had communities composed of Jews and non-Jews in a variety of combinations. After the war there was far less room for this. The communities became less diversified, the boundaries more sharply drawn.

Several measures taken by the rabbis after the war to delineate Judaism have been mentioned. We find repercussions of this in the New Testament. In the Gospel of Matthew, Jesus says, "But you are not to be called rabbi, for you have one teacher." This must reflect a postwar situation. The community of Matthew reacted in this way against the authority of the Pharisees, who now let themselves be "called rabbi." The warning that they will "flog you in their synagogues" must be seen in the same light.

This evokes the image of Jews from the church of Matthew who had been taking part in synagogue prayers but who could do so no longer. Many of them had perhaps also been in contact with non-Jewish Christians. That too must have become difficult indeed. (Matthew 23:8; 10:17)

Extremely high tensions can be discerned in the Gospel of John. Three times it states bitterly that the followers of Jesus shall be "put out of the synagogue." In this Gospel, too, Jesus says that the father of the Jews is "the devil," to which they answer that he has an evil spirit. Occasionally we even get the impression that there were casualties in this conflict. An observation already made in connection with Jesus' trial becomes significant here: in John, Jesus and his followers are positioned squarely over against "the Jews." This is reminiscent of the situation at Antioch. In John, an anti-Jewish church reveals itself; some extreme situation clearly was involved. (John 8:44; 9:22; 12:42; 16:2)

Thus both the Jewish and the Christian camps became more uniform and the peripheries more clearly demarcated. The war of 132–135 stimulated this development. Jews were no longer allowed to live in Jerusalem, thus indirectly strengthening the position of the non-Jewish Christians. The church there had henceforth a non-Jewish bishop. After that time Christians writers exhibit a new self-awareness. It is necessary, however, to distinguish between a more external, *social* tension with the Jews and an anti-Jewish *theology*. Social contrasts are normal in such a climate, but anti-Jewish theology is present only when the contrasts were also doctrinally motivated.

Rabbinic Judaism shielded itself further against Jewish and non-Jewish Christians. This was a social delineation. Rabbinic literature contains passages in which the Christian interpretation of the Bible is contested or Jesus is maligned. These are generally rather mild by comparison with the vehement polemics against Judaism by the church fathers. Theological arguments that Christianity as such was a godless fallacy do not occur.

The *apostolic churches* now stood wholly separate from Judaism. Originally that did not always entail anti-Jewish theology. Such late second-century church fathers as Irenaeus of Lyons, Clement of Alexandria, and Justin Martyr presented few objections to Judaism with respect to content. They continued reading the Old Testament with conviction, and their sermons contain a variety of Jewish traditions of interpretation. They even observed certain dietary and purity rules that resembled those of Judaism. Nonetheless, they emphasized that Christians keep no Jewish commandments. They were therefore not theologically but *socially* opposed to Judaism.

From the second century onward, however, a strong anti-Jewish theology is in evidence in Asia Minor and the surrounding areas. For some reason, the conflict between Jews and Christians appears to have been more fierce in that region. Ignatius of Antioch in the southeastern portion has been mentioned. In addition, an Easter sermon of Melito, bishop of Sardis, has been preserved. Alongside of various Jewish traditions of interpretation, a clearly anti-Jewish theology can be heard in it. God has turned against "Israel" because it had killed "the king of Israel," and now God has turned toward "all the families of humankind" with his offer of salvation. How tense relationships were becomes clear from a story about the martyrdom of Polycarp, a bishop of Smyrna, close to Sardis. According to the story, the Jews from his city zealously helped to drag wood to the stake. This certainly *could* have occurred. As mentioned above, occasional persecution of Christians by the Roman government of Asia Minor did occur. The Jews could have used such an occasion to improve their position in respect to their Christian "competitors." (p. 94)

It appears from other sources that at the end of the second century John was the favorite Gospel in Asia Minor. Along with points made above, this suggests that this Gospel may have originated there. In the following chapter I consider whether we can speak of anti-Jewish theology in John.

After the second century, anti-Jewish theology gradually developed outside of Asia Minor as well. The break with Judaism became no longer merely a social reality, but also a *theological necessity*. As though in and of itself, the idea that God had rejected his people came to the fore. Passages from the prophets in which Israel's disobedience is criticized were readily available. The promises of redemption that occur alongside of them were just as easily transferred to the church. Thus the Old Testament came to be read and interpreted in an anti-Jewish way. The same occurred with the numerous Jewish elements in the liturgy and with the retelling of Jesus' words and deeds in the Gospels. The church preserved all of these Jewish elements of tradition but interpreted them in an anti-Jewish way. The anti-Jewish theology meant that these elements *must* be thus understood. As this conviction became more self-evident and less conscious, its effect became the stronger.

So the opposition between rabbinic Judaism and the apostolic, anti-Jewish church worsened. The various Jewish Christians came to stand alone between the two fronts. Their isolation occasioned disintegration and extremism. Embattled by both sides, they were finally to disappear from history.

8

The Writings of
the New Testament

The New Testament is the key in the question of Jesus and Judaism. The attitude toward the Jews reflected in it is a most essential element. Jesus was a Jew, and he understood his calling wholly within the context of Judaism. The main issue at his arrest and trial was his meaning within Israel's history. After Easter as well, his followers testified to his significance primarily within the framework of that history.

The fact that many non-Jews joined the church did nothing to change this. What did change was *their attitude* toward the Jews. Here and there, an anti-Jewish reading of the Christian gospel gradually developed. The New Testament contains traces of this development. It appears that we cannot use this main witness uncritically. The time has come to describe this document as a whole and to indicate how it can be used.

In this chapter I survey the attitude of the writings of the New Testament toward the Jews. Where do we find anti-Judaism, and where do we not? In my final chapter I take up the question of how devoted readers of the New Testament should deal with the findings.

A Unity?

In the following survey, considerable differences come to light. In its attitude toward the Jews, the New Testament is far from uniform. This fact in itself requires separate attention.

Christians for a long time have become accustomed to reading the New Testament as having a unified perspective. Mutual differences were acknowledged but were read as expressions of the multifaceted richness of the Spirit. In the nineteenth century the awareness that the New Testament comprises different writings, each with its own historical background, began to emerge. Often this insight was viewed as an encroachment on the authority of the New Testament. But such a view is not necessary. Historical plurality need not be an impediment to reading the New Testament as a unity. This becomes apparent when we observe the development of these writings.

The totality of biblical writings is called the *canon*, from the Greek word for "rule," meaning rule of faith or of reading. More precisely, the canon identifies the books that are read *aloud* in the churches, the ones that are thus "canonical." These expressions do not necessarily imply an institution that made decisions with unquestioned authority (such a notion more accurately describes the church of the Middle Ages). In antiquity, matters were not so centrally regulated. Which books came to be read aloud arose from the practice of reading itself. To some extent, external disputes also played a role, such as the dispute with the Gnostics. Consensus concerning the canon emerged gradually and was never final and definitive. There are still churches that do not read the Revelation of John aloud. At the end of the second century, in Rome it appeared that even the Gospel of John might not make the canon!

The canon is thus a unity that has grown and evolved. The contents of the various writings show this as well. The Gospel of John employs an entirely different language of faith from that of Matthew, Mark, and Luke. Distinct mentalities and particular types of communities are reflected. Another example is the difference on faith and works in the Epistle of James compared with the letters of Paul. Nonetheless, the church reads both of these divergent writings. In its final form, the New Testament can be seen as a river nourished by rivulets from many separate valleys.

The developed unity is, however, a fact, and not only a fact of the past. The unity is constituted by the actual reading of the texts by the church and its members in the liturgy of the community and the prayers of the individual. By reading the Bible year by year, one comes to view those divergent texts as a whole. While being read, they become "our" texts, and we become characters in the story being read. We link ourselves to the texts and the texts are linked to one another, and a unity thereby emerges.

The church's reading practice does not, however, erase the differences. The plurality is on paper, the unity in the mind. The effect of this should not be underestimated. As though self-evident, we assume images from John while reading Luke, or we supplement Matthew from Paul. It is therefore necessary to open ourselves consciously to the differences in the writings of the New Testament. In a critical and historical approach, the differences are even more important.

Such an approach is imperative here. I have observed how Jews and Christians separately hedged themselves in after the war with Rome. The church even developed an anti-Jewish theology. In doing so, it appealed continually to the New Testament. That is why we must know whether and where such things are to be found in the New Testament. We need a critical and a historical overview of the attitude toward the Jews taken in the New Testament writings. Differences within a single text are also highly significant.

In Chapter 5 above I argued that such differences come clearly to the fore in the reports of Jesus' trial. This will be a fixed point of reference in the following survey.

Another such point is the Sabbath. Both Jews and non-Jews have always viewed the Sabbath as a prominent part of Jewish law and Jewish life. Differences on this point are telling in respect to the attitude toward Judaism. I have noted Jesus' own opinion. I now look at the attitude of the various authors of the New Testament. (p. 41)

Mark

Like all Gospels, Mark dates from after the war against Rome, but it is still the oldest Gospel. It clearly takes the situation of non-Jews into account. Thus, for example, the prohibition of divorce is adjusted to the non-Jewish legal situation in which the woman could take the initiative. Jesus' teachings are relatively sparsely quoted in Mark, and there are not many typically Jewish expressions. The emphasis is on stories of Jesus performing wonders and of his suffering. As a whole Mark is easy to conceive of as intended for non-Jewish Christians, for example, those in Rome. There are few traces of a breach in the relationship between Jews and non-Jews. (Mark 10:12)

The story of Jesus' suffering takes up almost half of Mark. It is striking that the Pharisees are mentioned only once in Mark's passion narrative, and on that occasion they were surprised at Jesus' intelligent answer to their question. Jesus' opponents were the chief priests and their assistants; they acted as Jesus' enemies, condemned him, and turned him over to Pilate. Pilate himself is described relatively neutrally as a cynical Roman administrator who with amazement observed the excitement of the chief priests about this strange prophet. (Mark 12:13)

Mark contains two stories with a discussion about the Sabbath, both times with the Pharisees. In the first, on the Sabbath Jesus' disciples plucked heads of grain while walking through the fields. The Jews had vastly divergent opinions about such cases. The Pharisees in the story thought it was not permitted; Jesus thought it was. He cited a saying that underscores this: "The Sabbath was made for humankind, and not humankind for the Sabbath." This is an internal Jewish discussion. As we have observed, this saying is also quoted in rabbinic writings, where it is used even more explicitly to underpin the position that the care for human life has precedence over the keeping of the Sabbath. (Mark 2:23; p. 41)

In the second story, Jesus healed someone on the Sabbath. First, he posed a question that must have been quite familiar to the Pharisees: "Is it lawful to do good or to do harm on the sabbath?" In rabbinic writings, the principle holds: "Care for life supersedes the Sabbath." This would have been valid only in a figurative sense, for the man was not in mortal danger. But the Pharisees must have sincerely supported the principle of care for life. While healing the man, Jesus apparently did not commit a forbidden act. The man involved had a "withered hand," an ailment whose nature remains unclear. Jesus merely said to him that he should stretch forth his arm, and the man was healed. (Mark 3:4)

A remarkable statement now follows: "The Pharisees went out and immediately conspired with the Herodians against him, how to destroy

him." Thus the Pharisees would have him killed because of a minute transgression of the Sabbath. Comparison with ancient Jewish sources shows
that this cannot be historically correct. It is true that the law of Moses
prescribes that transgressors of the Sabbath were to be stoned. This was,
however, not practiced in Jesus' time. Even the strictest group, the Essenes,
did not demand the death penalty for desecration of the Sabbath. The
Dead Sea Scrolls speak only of excommunication. The Pharisees' reaction
portrayed here is an exaggeration. A comparison with Luke's version of
the story makes this even more apparent. (Mark 3:6; Numbers 15:35)

Mark's statement about the Pharisees' plot suggests a non-Jewish
church that after the war had come into fierce conflict with the Jews. It is
significant that the Pharisees in this story react far more aggressively to
Jesus than in the whole passion narrative in this Gospel. Mark 3:6 thus
remains an exception within Mark. (p. 112)

Matthew

Matthew is based on Mark; almost all of the Markan material recurs
here. Yet Matthew is considerably longer. The difference lies primarily
in the additional teachings of Jesus that make up five "discourses." The
first and most important is the Sermon on the Mount. In these passages,
many Jewish expressions occur. Jesus speaks, for example, of the "kingdom
of heaven," an expression that also occurs in rabbinic literature, where
"heaven" is a circumlocution for God. Elsewhere in the New Testament
we consistently find "kingdom of God," apparently a "translation" for non-
Jewish readers. (Matthew 5:3)

One important aspect of Matthew is that these passages depict Jesus
as a typical Jewish teacher. In the Sermon on the Mount, for example, he
said, "Do not think that I have come to abolish the law or the prophets;
I have come not to abolish but to fulfill," and that even "the least of these
commandments" should be kept. These expressions occur in rabbinic literature as well. Consistent with this, when relating to non-Jews, Jesus said
that he was "sent only to the lost sheep of the house of Israel." He thus
considered himself to be called to preach to Jews only. In these portions
of Matthew, a clearly Jewish-Christian standpoint comes to the fore. It is

expressed characteristically in the saying about the "scribe who has been trained for the kingdom of heaven" who "brings out of his treasure what is new and what is old." (Matthew 5:17; 15:24; 13:52)

Precisely in such contexts we also find a sharp conflict with the Pharisees. Jesus admonished his followers that their righteousness must exceed that of the scribes and Pharisees. One of Jesus' speeches even consists entirely of accusations against "scribes and Pharisees, hypocrites." Explicitly diverging from Mark, Matthew brings the conflict with the Pharisees into the passion narrative. One of the charges is that the Pharisees let themselves be called "rabbi," which Jesus forbids for his followers. This, too, suggests a Jewish church that had come into conflict with the Pharisaic leaders after the war. It was only then that the Pharisees began to use the expression "rabbi" as a fixed title for scholars of the law. We can, therefore, characterize such texts as anti-Pharisaic. (Matthew 5:20; 23:13; pp. 61, 98)

The development of the Gospel of Matthew did not, however, stop here. Scattered throughout it we also find traces of a final, anti-Jewish reworking of the material. One example is the story of the Roman centurion from Capernaum. He approached Jesus with the firm belief that Jesus could heal his sick servant. Jesus praised the commander, saying, "In no one in Israel have I found such faith." He went on, however, to say that "many will come from east and west and will eat with Abraham and Isaac and Jacob in the kingdom of heaven"—a designation of future bliss—but that "the heirs of the kingdom will be thrown into the outer darkness." This conclusion diverges strongly from Luke's version of the story. Moreover, Jesus told a parable of tenants who refused to pay the rent for their vineyard and who killed the owner's son. In contrast to the version in Mark and Luke, Jesus here told this parable to "chief priests *and the Pharisees*" and added, "The kingdom of God will be taken away from you and given to *a people* that produces the fruits of the kingdom." This is a reflection of a church reacting against the Jewish people. (Matthew 8:11; 21:43; pp. 66, 117)

This final shift is observable in the passion narrative as well. The chief priests together with *the Pharisees* try to do away with Jesus. In contrast, Pilate is depicted as a well-meaning administrator who listened to his pious wife, who had been warned in a dream to do Jesus no harm. "The people as a whole," however, shouted to have Jesus executed with the words: "His blood be on us and our children." (Matthew 12:14; 27:25; p. 62)

The final result is confusing. Matthew exhibits two faces: *Jewish-Christian and anti-Jewish*. The two aspects can be explained by assuming that the Gospel went through a lengthy process of development. We can conceive of it as follows. The Gospel was composed within a Jewish church by adding Jewish-Christian teaching material to Mark. After the war with Rome, this church came into conflict with the synagogue, and, as a result, the role of the Pharisees was given a negative accent. Finally, the Gospel ended up in a strictly non-Jewish church where generalized anti-Jewish tendencies had their effect. This must have been toward the end of the first century. Scenes like that of Pilate's pious wife suggest circles related to the Roman army.

John

The Fourth Gospel uses its own distinct language, thus testifying to a separate development. It also exhibits a quite closed world of faith. Jesus and his disciples stand as shining examples of light in stark contrast to a world of darkness. A central figure is the disciple "whom Jesus loved," one closer to Jesus than Peter is. In the final chapter this disciple is presented as the most important "witness" to the preceding material. From antiquity, attempts have been made to identify the beloved disciple as Lazarus or—more frequently—John, the apostle. Since then many have referred to this document as "the Gospel according to John." This, however, cannot be correct. The narrator remains anonymous, and in one place is referred to as different from the "beloved" disciple (21:24). At the same time, he gives the impression of being so close to Jesus that he can explain *what Jesus actually intended*. (John 20:3; p. 90)

The Fourth Gospel provides an entirely idiosyncratic view of Jesus. This appears to be done consciously, for the narrator gives the impression of being familiar with the other Gospels. He summons the reader, as it were, to look more deeply and to understand more profoundly. The story of Nicodemus, a Pharisee who came by night to talk to Jesus, brings this out. Nicodemus was sympathetic to Jesus, as is seen later, when he argued for an honest trial for Jesus and when after the crucifixion he assisted with Jesus' burial. The narrator shows, however, that in the conversation by night Nicodemus did not understand Jesus. Jesus said, "Are you a teacher of Israel, and yet you do not understand these things?" The reader is invited to look more deeply than Nicodemus did. (John 3:10)

In this Gospel Jesus is seen not only as God's "only Son"; he is also the creative Word (Greek: *logos*) of God who is himself "God," the Word that became flesh. Such "theologizing" language is often viewed as being un-Jewish; Judaism, after all, maintained a strict separation between God and human. Indeed, rabbinic literature usually does not express itself in this manner. Nonetheless, there were Jews at that time who used comparable language when speaking about God and his Word, an important example of which is Philo of Alexandria. Rabbis such as Akiba are also reported to have had mystical experiences in which the human came very close to God. John's theological language concerning Jesus is therefore in itself not un-Jewish. (John 1:1)

There is, however, a deep rift between this Gospel and Judaism on the issue of the Sabbath. Again, two stories about the Sabbath occur. In one, Jesus ordered a healed man to carry his sleeping mat—on the Sabbath! In the other story, Jesus made a kind of medicine on the Sabbath for someone who had been blind all his life. To the extent that we can verify this, even the most moderate Pharisees considered both of these actions to be forbidden on the Sabbath. Jesus justified his position with the words that he was God's Son, who, just as his Father, works on this day. According to this Gospel, Jesus thus *consciously* transgressed the Sabbath rules that were in force. The reaction speaks volumes: "For this reason the Jews were seeking all the more to kill him, because he was not only breaking the Sabbath, but was also calling God his own Father, thereby making himself equal to God." (John 5:8, 18; 9:6)

Several things occur here at the same time. As in Mark and Matthew, Jesus' opponents wanted to kill him because of his breaking of the Sabbath, but only in John is there actually a case of willful transgression. The accusation is added that Jesus called himself God's Son. In Mark and Luke, this was a charge leveled at him by the high priest and his cohorts, consistent with their presumably Sadducean background. The Sadducees would have nothing of Jesus' preaching about the coming Son of Man and the imminent kingdom of God. In John, however, the accusation is ascribed to "the Jews" in general. Thus this Gospel is a reaction against the Jews who adhere to the commandments concerning the Sabbath and who do not see that Jesus as God's Son stands above the Sabbath. (John 1:17; p. 68).

Worse still, in this Gospel Jesus' enemies are consistently designated as "the Jews." It becomes clear that the evangelist retold his story from a later perspective. Differences between Jesus' various opponents are reduced practically to nothing. We can be sure about this because it was not done entirely consistently; at times in one verse specific antagonists of Jesus are mentioned who in another verse are lumped together as "the Jews." The story of Jesus' trial makes this clear. The plan to kill Jesus was conceived by "the chief priests" together with "the Pharisees." Later, these same conspirators are indicated as "the Jews." Further, the soldiers who capture Jesus are first called "police from the chief priests and Pharisees" but later "the Jewish police." Finally, "the Jews" are the ones who, on the basis of "their law," turned Jesus over to Pilate to have him crucified. (John 11:47, 57; 18:3; 18:12)

All of this is evidence of a community that had come to a complete break with the Jews. In this Gospel we find the expression that the followers of Jesus are "put out of the synagogue" by the "Pharisees" or "the Jews." Even "the Jews who had come to believe in him" are attacked. This must refer to Jewish Christians. When they boasted of having Abraham as their forefather, Jesus said that they were descended from the devil. Jewish Christians who held on to their lineage are presented as diabolical antagonists! (John 8:44, 48; 9:22; 8:31)

I noted in the previous chapter that an anti-Jewish theology first came to the fore in Asia Minor and surroundings. It was precisely there that the Gospel of John was held in honor at the end of the second century. It is therefore reasonable to localize the strong anti-Jewish attitude of John in that area as well. A partial confirmation of this is that church tradition associates the Gospel with the city of Ephesus, on the west coast of Asia Minor. The anti-Jewish attitude of the Gospel is clear from its indiscriminate designation of Jesus' enemies as "the Jews." Indeed we encounter here the rudiments of anti-Jewish theology: the presentation of Jewish Christians as diabolical and the abolition of the Sabbath by Jesus as God's Son.

The Gospel of John is the earliest document containing these phenomena. (p. 100)

Nonetheless, this is not the whole story. The Gospel of John originated in Jewish-Christian surroundings as well and contains many traditional elements from those circles. One of the arguments with which Jesus supported his acting on the Sabbath reveals this. He said that it is like circumcision, which is performed on the eighth day after birth even if that happens to be a Sabbath. The Sabbath is thus put aside in order to keep the law of Moses. This same argument is brought forward by a rabbi in order to underpin that preservation of life supersedes the keeping of the Sabbath. The argument is based on the premise that one must keep the law of Moses. But this is in contrast to the Gospel as a whole; a Jewish-Christian tradition is preserved within the anti-Jewish text. (John 7:23; p. 41)

In spite of all this, and without danger of being misunderstood, I conclude by referring to the quiet beauty that emanates from the Gospel of John. There is no space here to expound on images such as light, the shepherd, and the vine. Certainly, in such as these we have one of the reasons why this is the most beloved Gospel.

Luke and Acts

The Gospel of Luke, too, is based on Mark. It is written by the same author as the Acts of the Apostles. This is clear, among other things, from his prefaces to both documents. An ancient church tradition identifies the author as Luke, a non-Jewish physician from Antioch and co-worker of Paul, mentioned by the apostle himself. There is no definitive confirmation of this tradition, but there is also little against it. In any case, "Luke" shows himself to be an admirer of Paul. (Luke 1:1; Acts 1:1; Colossians 4:14)

With regard to the Sabbath, the author has a frankly positive attitude toward Jews and Judaism. His Gospel contains more stories about the Sabbath than any other Gospel; besides the two stories from Mark there are three others. In none of these did Jesus act counter to Pharisaic opinion. The Pharisees did not feel comfortable with his behavior, but they could accuse him of nothing. Time and again they remained in confused silence. This is most striking after the healing of the man with the withered hand. In Matthew and Mark the Pharisees' reaction is that they wanted to kill Jesus. In Luke we read, "They were filled with fury and discussed with one another what they might do to Jesus." Jesus' disciples respected the Sabbath as well. The women who wanted to care for the body of Jesus after the crucifixion waited until the Sabbath was past "according to the commandment." (Luke 6:11; 13:17; 14:6; 23:56)

The author has a remarkably positive view of Judaism. He emphasizes how, after the birth of their son, Jesus' parents kept the Jewish customs according to "the law of the Lord." Nonetheless, the author also registers a number of conflicts between Jesus and the Pharisees, as well as between Paul and many synagogues. Jesus thought the Pharisees to be "lovers of money"; Paul clashed various times with synagogue elders. Still, Jesus three times enjoyed hospitality in the house of a Pharisee—a detail we are told only in Luke. In spite of all the conflicts, Paul contended to the end that he had "no charge to bring against my nation." He also kept the commandments as though that were a matter of course. (Luke 2:21; 16:14; Acts 13:46; 28:19)

Except for the points already mentioned, the Pharisees do not have a negative role in these Luke and Acts. They had an open but distant relationship to Jesus. Concerned for his life, several Pharisees came to Jesus to warn him that Herod Antipas wanted to kill him! In Acts the prominent Pharisee Gamaliel pleaded that Jesus' apostles be set free. The same Pharisee is later mentioned as Paul's former teacher. The author underscores that it was not the Pharisees but the Sadducees who were the mortal enemies of Jesus and his disciples. (Luke 7:36; 11:37; 13:31; 14:1; Acts 5:38; 22:3)

Just like Mark, this author does not consider the Pharisees to blame for Jesus' condemnation. This is the more remarkable because he—this time diverging from Mark—plainly betrays a tendency to exonerate Pilate. For the rest, his description of the trial is matter-of-fact and many-sided. The high priest and his people sentenced Jesus for blasphemy in accordance with their Sadducean perspectives. The Pharisees were not involved in the trial. When the high priest later accused Jesus' disciples, the Pharisees made a plea for moderation. (p. 72)

The author also gives non-Jews ample attention. As in Matthew, in Luke we find the story of the centurion from Capernaum, but an entirely different conclusion is given. We are told that the commander was in good standing with the Jews and had helped build the local synagogue. Similar things are said of Cornelius, the centurion from Caesarea who came to believe through Peter. He was one of the many non-Jews who were attracted to Judaism without actually joining it. Paul found his best audience among such so-called God-fearers. The author makes it clear that this did not mean that these people also became Jews. At a gathering of the apostles in Jerusalem it was agreed that non-Jewish Christians need only keep certain basic commandments. (Luke 7:5; Acts 10:2; pp. 88, 107)

The author does note that Paul's preaching was generally rejected by the synagogues in the diaspora. A few times on such an occasion the apostle exclaimed that "we are now turning to the Gentiles." But, through all this the author maintains his consistent appreciation of the Jewish law and the Pharisees. The author thus must not have considered Paul's exclamations to be in conflict with this. Probably writing toward the end of the first century, he appears to have in mind the fact that most of the synagogues had rejected the gospel. Yet he seems quietly to maintain the hope of improved relationships. Especially the conclusion of Acts strengthens this surmise. Before Paul decided definitely to turn to the non-Jews, the leaders of the Jewish congregation in Rome departed from him "while they disagreed with each other" concerning his message. (Acts 13:46; 18:6; 28:25)

In short, the two books of this author relate how the gospel emerged in the pious Jewish environment of Jesus, spread among the Jews, and thereafter attracted many non-Jews throughout the whole world—without giving up the original bond with the Jews. The preaching of the gospel to all peoples continued to be based on an open relationship with Jews and Judaism.

This is a remarkable message, in particular given the time of its writing. During the same time, Mark, Matthew, and John were reworked in an anti-Jewish direction. The account of Luke and Acts is also relevant for Christians in our time. It shows how one can remain faithful to the gospel without continuing a negative attitude toward the Jews.

Paul

Paul's letters all date from the end of the 40s to the end of the 50s. They testify in various ways to the growing tensions between Jews and non-Jews that were felt also within the churches. We must treat them as real letters: each letter addresses a unique situation that usually is indicated only indirectly. We remember also that when Paul used similar concepts in different letters, he was not necessarily dealing with the same issue.

Yet there is one theme that recurs in most of the letters, namely, that the *church is one body* that includes both Jewish and non-Jewish members. Paul expressed this in his "rule in all the churches": each member must remain in the calling in which he or she was called. This rule was threatened wherever either Christians were pressured to become Jews or when Jewish Christians were excluded. Such things did occur. In his letters to Galatia, Philippi, and Colossae and in 2 Corinthians, Paul defended himself against those who held to the idea of an exclusively Jewish church. In the letter to Rome the case was the opposite, and he combated the efforts to maintain an exclusively non-Jewish church. (1 Corinthians 7:17; p. 88)

The Sabbath is mentioned in two letters, in both cases in connection with the relationship between Jews and non-Jews. One of the letters was intended for the church at Colossae, a city in Asia Minor. Some there thought that Christians should follow the Jewish law. Paul protested. It would be a violation of freedom for followers of Jesus to be exclusively either Jewish or non-Jewish. Among the disputed points was the Sabbath. But, the apostle wrote, Sabbath and dietary rules are mere "shadows" of the essence of the matter. What it is really about is "the body," namely, Christ. Jewish and non-Jewish believers are one in that body. "There is no longer Greek and Jew, circumcised and uncircumcised. . . ." (Colossians 2:17; 3:11)

He argued for the same position in his letter to the church in Rome, although with the opposite reasoning. In Rome, the non-Jewish Christians had come to resent the customs of their Jewish brothers and sisters. Again, Paul pleaded for room for differences: "Some judge one day to be better than another, while others judge all days to be alike. Let all be fully convinced in their minds." This letter also was written at the end of the 50s. While Jewish and non-Jewish Christians were being driven apart, Paul tried with all his might to keep them within one church. (Romans 14:5)

It is therefore a misconception to think that Paul considered the Jewish law to be abolished or that he set aside bothersome rules such as the Sabbath and dietary regulations. These essential components of Jewish life remained in force—for Jewish believers—even though Paul perhaps would interpret certain details more freely than others would. Paul occasionally made critical comments about the law, indicating that living according to the Jewish law does not create a utopia on earth. Some Jews urged others to believe that, and some non-Jews were eager to accept it. Life according to the law entails human endeavor, including its failures. One is not "justified" by this. Paul borrowed this peculiar expression from the story of Abraham. Abraham was justified because of his faith. Circumcision followed only some time later as a "seal" of his faith. Therefore, he could become the "ancestor of all who believe," both Jewish and non-Jewish. (Genesis 15:6; 17:1; Romans 4:10)

It is often said that Paul's Christology exceeds the bounds of Judaism. Yet he does nothing more than apply biblical expressions to the figure of Jesus. Often he transparently borrowed expressions from early Christian tradition. Thus, he viewed Jesus as the one in whose being the kingdom of God had already dawned, as a "firstborn within a large family," a "firstborn of all creation; for in him all things in heaven and on earth were created." Like the Gospel of John and certain ancient Jewish traditions, Paul saw the Messiah as the creative Word of God, or as the Son of Man, the heavenly Savior in human form. The latter comes out in a hymn of praise to Jesus that he cites: "Who, though he was in the form of God . . . emptied himself, taking the form of a slave, being born in human likeness." Christ the firstborn, however, remains subject to God. A comparable Christology can be found in the Epistle of Jude. Jesus is Lord and Christ but in the end remains subject to the Father of all. (Romans 8:29; Colossians 1:15; Philippians 2:6; 1 Corinthians 15:28; Jude 25)

As I mentioned above, each of Paul's letters has a unique occasion and purpose. Within his churches the relationship of the converts to the Jews was varied and was also subject to strong shifts. Thus Paul could make seemingly conflicting statements about the Jews. A sharp condemnation of the Jews occurs in the first letter to the young church in Thessalonica. According to Acts, the Jews there had vehemently resisted Paul's preaching. In this they were successful in influencing many non-Jews. Paul was apparently afraid that the new members of the church would thereby

abandon their faith. In that context he was extremely agitated in his accusations against the Jews in Judea: They have "killed both the Lord Jesus
and the prophets . . . , they displease God . . . by hindering us from speaking to the Gentiles. . . . God's wrath has overtaken them at last." (1 Thessalonians 2:14; Acts 17:5)

These are certainly not innocent statements, and attempts to show
that these are not Paul's own words are unconvincing. Considering other
texts from Paul, however, it becomes apparent that these words must be
interpreted in their specific context.

A number of years later Paul expressed himself quite differently. In
Romans he presented a well-deliberated exposition about the essence of
a church that was experiencing tensions between Jews and non-Jews. The
slogan here is justification by faith, "to the Jew first and also to the Greek."
The order is important. Paul underscored that the Jews have a special
place in the church. God's covenant with them is, after all, irrevocable.
Non-Jews are therefore admonished to conduct themselves modestly
toward Jews and Jewish Christians. In exalted terms, repeatedly evoking
the image of the people of Israel before Sinai, Paul ends his comments on
this question with the statement that in the end "all Israel will be saved."
(Romans 1:16; 11:26)

These words have lost none of their prophetic impact for Christian
churches. They show also that the outburst in the letter to Thessalonica
should not be taken as absolute. When Paul wrote those objectionable
words, he was aflame with holy anger: his work in northern Greece was
in danger of being ruined. He compared Greek resistance to the gospel
in that area with the Jewish opposition in Judea. In a shocking way he
used the Judean Jews as a negative example, although he apparently did
not intend by this to condemn all Jews. Furthermore, his presentation is
utterly one-sided. He was silent about a significant point that he elsewhere
frankly admitted, namely, that he himself had belonged to the persecutors
of the churches in Judea. (Galatians 1:13; Philippians 3:6; 1 Corinthians
15:9)

With this critique we are not yet finished with Paul's outburst against
the Judean Jews. His letter came to belong to the core of the New Testament and thus to the canon of the apostolic churches. The vehement
explosion in Thessalonians fit well into their anti-Jewish manner of reading, but the deliberate, studied language of Romans did not. The tempta-

tion was great to read the passage in Thessalonians outside of its concrete context and to make it into a general condemnation of the Jews. If only Paul had not written those words!

We can, however, establish something else as well. The picture of Paul in Acts is in line with Romans, not with 1 Thessalonians. Acts portrays Paul as passionately concerned about his people while at the same time firmly supporting preaching to non-Jews. The faithfulness of the Jews to the law is a self-evident part of this passion. Within the apostolic churches, this interpretation did not prevail over the anti-Jewish reading of Paul. In part, this had to do with external circumstances. But there is no reason why we today should not draw attention to this interpretation.

Jewish-Christian Writings

Finally, there is a group of New Testament texts of unique value—writings from Jewish churches. Their uniqueness lies in the fact that hardly any other documentation from Jewish Christians has been preserved. Crushed between rabbinic Judaism and non-Jewish Christianity, the Jewish Christians finally disappeared from history, and with them their writings. Church fathers mention Jewish-Christian Gospels and occasionally quote from them. Further, scholars find here and there a Jewish-Christian source incorporated into an apostolic-Christian writing. But this appears to be the extent of it.

Quite near the end of the New Testament, however, there are four documents that can be considered to originate from Jewish churches. The fact that they are placed toward the end is not accidental. Their inclusion in the canon was not at all a foregone conclusion. The last of the four, the Revelation of John, is still not accepted by some churches. Due to its "anti-Pauline" content, the Epistle of James was roundly criticized by Martin Luther. The Epistle to the Hebrews is the best known, precisely because of its supposed correspondence to Paul's thinking. This seems to be the criterion. The New Testament is the canon of the apostolic non-Jewish churches. In this, besides the four Gospels, the letters of Paul are the most important—with Paul read in an anti-Jewish manner.

The four Jewish-Christian writings are therefore the more valuable. The fact that they were included in the canon proves that Jewish elements in the Christian tradition were not totally suppressed. Besides, correspondences in content can reveal and illumine Jewish aspects of Paul and, for example, of Matthew.

The Epistle of Jude

The Epistle of Jude is perhaps the least known writing in the New Testament, although it contains matters certainly as interesting as the brief letter of Paul to Philemon. It was not written by the famous Paul but by a certain "Jude . . . brother of James." The writer warns of preachers who could lead Christians astray. These false teachers are designated by names of Old Testament reprobates such as Cain, Bileam, Korah, and the inhabitants of Sodom and Gomorrah. The author also cites other ancient Jewish writings such as 1 Enoch. Similar elements are well known from the Qumran scrolls and other writings from the Jewish homeland. Furthermore, the writer's view of Jesus corresponds to Paul's but also contains unique elements. He gives Jesus the Old Testament title of "Master." These aspects indicate that the letter originated in some church in the Jewish homeland. It is thus not impossible that the James of whom the author calls himself a brother was Jesus' oldest brother. Paul calls the latter "the Lord's brother" and presents him as the leader of the church in Jerusalem. The writer of this short letter might then be none other than Jude or Judah, their younger brother. (Galatians 1:19; Mark 6:3)

The Epistle of James

The Epistle of James could also be from the Jewish homeland. It is composed in good Greek but exhibits a constant switching of motifs reminiscent of the style of certain pious Jewish tractates. The recurrent warning against slander and exploitation of poor peasants brings to mind the same. There is a certain affinity with the Jewish-Christian material in Matthew. As to provenance, one could think of the Jewish homeland or a bordering agrarian territory. Unique within ancient Christian literature is the designation of the meetings of the readers as "your synagogue"—although modern translations often obscure this (NRSV: "your assembly"). The rhetoric of James resembles the popular preaching style that we see also in Paul's letter to the Romans: "Do you want to be shown, you senseless person, that faith apart from works is barren?" (James 2:2, 20; Romans 2:3)

The contents also remind us of Romans: "Was not our ancestor Abraham justified by works when he offered his son Isaac on the altar?" This can even be read as a critical comment on the Epistle to the Romans: "A person is justified by works and not by faith alone." What is the writer's intention? He addresses his letter "to the twelve tribes in the Dispersion." Commentators have usually read that as a metaphorical reference to the church, but the image of the twelve tribes might rather suggest a Jewish-Christian environment. Its intention would then be to oppose a radical interpretation of Paul: it is *not* the case that "justification by faith" makes the Jewish law superfluous! The author would be then either James himself or someone writing in his name who wanted to keep Jewish Christians from an anti-Jewish reading of Paul. (James 2:21, 24; p. 86)

The Epistle to the Hebrews

The Epistle to the Hebrews has some resemblance to Paul, but already in antiquity some Christians attributed it to someone else. The author's "spiritual" explanation of the temple and of Jesus as the heavenly high priest is well known. The earthly sanctuary with its rituals, he says, is but a "shadow of the heavenly one"—an expression reminiscent of Paul. The question is how this should be read. The traditional interpretation, which also reads Paul in an anti-Jewish manner, sees in this the notion that the "ceremonial law" of the Jews is abolished at the death of Jesus. (Hebrew 8:5; p. 117)

It is significant, however, that the author wrote this while the temple in Jerusalem apparently was still functioning. Jesus is depicted as sitting in heaven on God's right hand, as a spiritual high priest "according to the order of Melchizedek." He serves in the heavenly temple prepared by God's "hand." This alludes to biblical verses that were also explicitly quoted in Qumran. The Essenes boycotted the temple of Jerusalem, because there the law was not kept according to their interpretation of it. Having deserted Jerusalem, they spoke of a spiritual temple in heaven. Something similar is done by this author. Jesus is not a real priest: "If he were on earth, he would not be a priest at all, since there are priests who offer gifts according to the law." The earthly sanctuary is "a symbol of the present time, during which gifts and sacrifices are offered that cannot perfect the conscience of the worshiper." (Psalm 110:4; Exodus 15:17; Hebrews 7:11; 8:4; 9:9)

It thus appears that the author allows the temple in Jerusalem its literal value while looking for its spiritual sense in heaven, in Jesus at God's right hand. He speaks of the Sabbath in the same manner. This day of rest is kept by people on earth, but it is a reflection of the heavenly rest of the Creator on the seventh day. The thought-world of Hebrews is related not only to that of the Essenes but also to that of Philo of Alexandria, the philosopher-theologian who conjoined deep spiritual significance with the "superficial" letter of the law. The author of Hebrews saw the most profound meaning personified in Jesus. He could well have been a Jewish Christian from Alexandria. (Hebrews 4:9; Genesis 2:2; p. 25)

The Revelation of John

The Revelation of John is a Jewish-Christian writing with a somewhat different background. This is brought out in the "letters" that the writer addresses "in Jesus' name" to seven churches in western Asia Minor. He calls himself "John" and writes from the island of Patmos, on the coast of Asia Minor. Which John this is we do not know. Later tradition identifies him with the writer of the fourth Gospel, although the two have noticeably different styles. (Revelation 1:9)

The book contains a "revelation of Jesus Christ." Strife of gigantic proportions between the heavenly Jesus and the worldly ruler, Satan, is depicted in colorful and passionate images. There are also allusions to oppression of Christians under the Roman regime. The famous "number of the beast," 666, probably is a code for Nero, the emperor who in the 60s was the first to execute Christians. John wrote apparently at the end of the first century under Emperor Domitian, who likewise made life difficult for Christians. Domitian was thus seen as "Nero revived." In any event, John depicted the world in black and white: in opposition to Jesus, who reigns from heaven over his faithful ones on earth, stand the emperor of Rome and his servants as the devil's henchmen. The book encourages the believers from the perspective of the certainty of Jesus' victory. (Revelation 1:1; 13:18)

This type of writing was cherished in certain circles in the Jewish homeland, including in the sect of Qumran. The Epistle of Jude cites such a writing, namely 1 Enoch. John's "Revelation of Jesus Christ" is related to this genre and has an explicitly Jewish-Christian character. The core of the faithful ones of the heavenly Jesus are the "one hundred forty-four thousand . . . of the people of Israel," twelve thousand from each of the twelve tribes. Around these stand a "multitude that no one could count" from all the peoples of the earth. They are clothed in white raiment and praise God in his heavenly temple. This image occurs as well in the Epistle to the Hebrews. The new Jerusalem, which at the end descends from heaven, contains no temple—not a surprising thought after the destruction of Jerusalem in 70. The explanation that the white robes are "the righteous deeds of the saints" is again typically Jewish-Christian. (Revelation 7:4, 9; 19:8; p. 28)

It is apparently in this light that we should view the two sharp outbursts against "those who say that they are Jews and are not, but are a synagogue of Satan." They occur in the letters "from Jesus Christ" to the churches in Smyrna (Izmir) and Philadelphia. The identity of this "Satan" becomes clear by the fact that he threw several Christians from Smyrna "into prison"; he is the Roman government official. The writer, therefore, viewed the accused synagogues as collaborators with the Roman regime. It is not inconceivable that Jews at the end of the first century cooperated in campaigns against Christians. As we have seen, this is reported about Smyrna later, at the time of Polycarp. For the writer, the term "Jew" is not a term of abuse but a title of honor that the members of the accused synagogues do not deserve. (Revelation 2:9; 3:9; p. 100)

I have mentioned the conjecture that the Gospel of John was also written in Asia Minor. There, a vehement anti-Jewish position was supported by rudiments of anti-Jewish theology. Can the same be said of the Revelation of John? The Asia Minor location is certain in the latter case, and the time of writing is to all intents and purposes the same. Here, too, the opponents are depicted as diabolical. Nonetheless, the position chosen is not anti-Jewish. The opponents are not indiscriminately called "the Jews," as in the Fourth Gospel. They are people who "say that they are Jews and are not." They are not worthy of the name "Jews." The writer apparently means that this title of honor may be borne only by Jewish Christians who are true to their calling and do not bow to the diabolical cult of the emperor. A comparatively positive appeal to the name "Jew" can be found in Paul's writings. (Romans 2:29)

This difference between Revelation and the Gospel of John is crucial. It reminds us that, even after the war with Rome, Jewish Christians could make vehement outbursts against their Jewish opponents without becoming anti-Jewish.

The Readers of
the New Testament

I have called attenton to significant differences within and among the writings of the New Testament. An anti-Jewish attitude comes out in John and Matthew and at a few points in Mark. Alongside this, however, Matthew exhibits explicitly Jewish-Christian material. The Epistles of Jude and James and the Epistle to the Hebrews as well as the Revelation of John show themselves to be fully Jewish-Christian. Luke and Acts describe the spread of the gospel among non-Jews on the basis of continuity with Judaism. Finally, Paul in one passage raves against the Jews in Judea but elsewhere deliberately and thoughtfully speaks of the continuing calling of "all Israel."

What are we to do with these differences? I focus now on the *readers*— an elusive term until we realize and specify who they are. The New Testament is not only the key witness in the question of Jesus and the Jews but also the core document of the Christian church in its various forms. This is common knowledge. One who picks up the New Testament is at least indirectly confronted with the church. What readers do with the different attitudes toward the Jews in the New Testament is therefore related to their attitude toward the church.

This is the reverse of what I observed at the beginning of the preceding chapter. The various writings of the New Testament became a unity through the process of being read together in the church, which thereby made these writings its own. The unity of these writings is derived from their appropriation by the church. Emphasizing the differences can be felt to be an infringement on or denigration of the "Holy Scripture" of the church. This same attitude makes it difficult to recognize incongruities, allow doubts, or enter into discussion.

The New Testament is not available with no strings attached. It is invisibly enshrouded in attitudes and opinions that from antiquity have determined the manner in which the New Testament is read. The shrouds are difficult to remove. They are indicated by a number of code words: one reads the New Testament in *faith*, as *Holy Scripture*, in the context of the *church*, and so on. Even when one does not take the whole package, these attitudes and notions must be challenged, and thus they still have their effect.

The situation is comparable to codes under which all sorts of transactions are programmed in the modern world. Without the right codes at the right moment we are denied access and can accomplish nothing. In this final chapter I try to decode the most important codes that "program" the reading of the New Testament. In this I note also their Jewish background. We can thus see how the codes originally worked and how they can be reprogrammed.

I hope thereby to close this book in an open-ended manner, without passing theological judgments or providing moral guidelines. It is up to the reader to sort out the different attitudes toward the Jews in the New Testament by activating the code words.

Faith

Everything in the New Testament is about "faith." The question is, *what*, exactly, does faith involve? Faith is something you "confess"; it is summarized in a "confession," a "creed." The most concise confession is to be found everywhere in the New Testament: Jesus Christ. Though usually understood as a name, it is also a confession. But two words should be added: "Jesus is the Christ," that is, Jesus is the Messiah. The core of the New Testament is the mini-confession, "Jesus is the Messiah." (p. 80)

This is precisely the focus of the discussion about Jesus' significance, the pivot around which the whole question of Jesus turns. At this point opinions diverge, among Jews then and now and in another way among non-Jews. It is, however, in the first place a Jewish discussion, for "Messiah" is originally a Jewish concept.

The discussion is as old as the confession. In an earlier chapter I considered the question John the Baptist put to Jesus, "Are you the one who is to come, or are we to wait for another?" John had been Jesus' teacher, and he did not reject Jesus right off. This makes his critical question the more eloquent. We have seen that there were many other Jews who posed the question whether Jesus should be called the Messiah. The core of Christian faith, the confession "Jesus is the Christ," was thus challenged from the beginning. (Luke 7:19; p. 45)

Not only has the belief that Jesus was the Messiah been contested but it is also by its nature contestable. Faith cannot exist without testing, and faith without doubt is superficial. The question of John may therefore not be silenced. It is a question from the inside.

In his answer to John's question, Jesus points to the "signs" of redemption that he had wrought: "Tell John what you have seen and heard: the blind receive their sight, the lame walk. . . ." This type of answer is appropriate in this context. In Jewish discussions about the coming of the Messiah, the question is always about the signs that would occur. In a religious dispute in Spain in the thirteenth century, the famous rabbi Nachmanides asked how Christians could say that Jesus is the Messiah. After all, in Isaiah it is written concerning the kingdom of the Messiah, when redemption dawns, "neither shall they learn war any more." Christians, however, did nothing but organize crusades! Nachmanides won the debate, and the Jews had rest for years to come. (Luke 7:22; Isaiah 2:4)

The crusades were indeed more a sign of the new power of Western Europe than of the success of Jesus' message. What about the "signs" that Jesus himself performed? What he did and said was reason enough for his disciples to believe that he was the Messiah. This is expressed toward the end of the Gospel of John: "Jesus did many other signs in the presence of his disciples, which are not written in this book. But these are written *so that you may come to believe that Jesus is the Messiah, the Son of God*." Most Jews, however, did not find Jesus' signs to be convincing. Nor did the young Pharisee Paul. He thought Jesus' teachings were a dangerous fallacy. Only later did he come to believe, he writes, "through a revelation of Jesus Christ." In other words, it became suddenly clear to him that Jesus was the Messiah. That is, of course, not a real answer; the basis of Paul's faith remains a mystery. (John 20:30; Galatians 1:12)

Perhaps that is always the case. What is there actually to be seen or heard? Is it not dependent on how you look and how you listen? Signs have significance only for those who can read them. Is that not true as well for the signs that you read in faith? For clarity we must broaden our field of vision.

The confession "Jesus is the Messiah" is the core of Christian faith, but at the same time it is a part of a much greater movement. Faith played a key role in Jesus' own message. Jesus began his public ministry with these words, "The time is fulfilled, and the kingdom of God has come near; repent, and *believe* in the good news." In faith Jesus saw this happening around him, and he summoned his disciples to follow him in that belief. Faith is so central to Jesus' own message that the sick appeared to be healed through their own faith. How often did he not say to one healed by him, "Your faith has saved you"! (Mark 1:14; 5:34; Luke 7:50; p. 36)

In Greek and in Hebrew, "faith" equals "trust," "confidence." The confidence that Jesus was the embodiment of the coming of God's kingdom gave the lame the power to straighten themselves. In turn, Jesus looked them straight in the eyes and took them by the hand. Without that trust of faith, nothing happens, and there is nothing to be seen. This is what Jesus himself described by the enigmatic reference to faith as a mustard seed. The evangelists each use that expression in their own manner to indicate the miraculous nature of faith. There is also a parable in which Jesus compares the coming of God's kingdom to a mustard seed, "the smallest of all the seeds on earth; yet when it is sown it grows up and becomes the greatest of all shrubs, and puts forth large branches, so that the birds of the air can make nests in its shade." According to Jesus, faith is assuming the trust to sow that insignificant seed. (Matthew 17:20; Luke 17:6; Mark 4:31)

In the broadest sense, faith is the trust that God cares for his creatures. Jesus said, "If God so clothes the grass of the field, which is alive today and tomorrow is thrown into the oven, will he not much more clothe you—

you of little faith?" Faith is the trust through which we can read the tiniest things as signs of God's care, as indications that his kingdom is nearby. Within that broad perspective, Jesus' own words and deeds can be read as signs. He himself can be seen as the incarnation of God's kingdom, as the promised Messiah. Against the backdrop of world history, he is as insignificant as the "grain of wheat [that] falls into the earth and dies." In a concealed manner he is precisely in this way "the firstborn of all creation." (Matthew 6:30; John 12:24; Colossians 1:15)

In their own way, for Paul, just as for James and for the rabbis, the "ancestor of all those who believe" is Abraham. Abraham heard God's voice giving him a commission and a promise, and he undertook the journey. Still he did not know where he was going. In this he became our ancestor: "Abraham believed God, and it was reckoned to him as righteousness." Again he heard God's voice, this time with the assignment to offer his only, beloved son. He did not understand this at all; this was the severest test of his faith. Again he undertook the journey in the trust that God would provide a solution. Faith following in Abraham's footsteps means entering into testing, daring to face the unknown, trusting that God has thus far led you on the right way. Faith is in trust embracing doubt. In this way "the righteous [shall] live by their faith." (Romans 4:3, 11; James 2:21; Genesis 12:1; 15:6; 22:1; Habakkuk 2:4)

Holy Scripture

The New Testament is part of the Bible or, as it has long been called, "Holy Scripture." For many Protestants this code word involves the Bible being "the infallible word of God." In other ways, also for many Roman Catholic and Eastern Orthodox believers, the authority of the Bible is inviolable. In what respect can we say that the Bible is "holy"?

The expression occurs but once in the whole Bible, in the solemn introduction of Paul's letter to the Romans: "The gospel of God, which he promised beforehand through his prophets in the *holy scriptures*. . . ." Usually the writers of the New Testament speak of "the writings," by which they mean nothing else than the books of the Old Testament. Ancient rabbinic writings also speak of "*holy* writings." By this they mean the books that were read aloud in the synagogue. That is what we are concerned with here. "Scripture" or the "scriptures" are called holy because they were read aloud in the congregation. This is more because of their function within the reading community than because of their contents. As explained in the previous chapter, the unity of the Scriptures is to be found here as well. It is a unity that is *read* by the community. (Romans 1:2; p. 103)

Protestants in particular are not used to noticing the reading community. They look rather to the thinking individual. That is why they tend to emphasize the contents of the biblical books more than the practice of the reading community. The track, however, goes dead here. Why is the story of the openly God-fearing Judith not "Holy Scripture" while that of Esther is, even though she serves God only in secret? Why are the profound counsels of Jesus Sirach not a part of Scripture while the skeptical sayings of Ecclesiastes are? Such is the case in the Hebrew canon, which was adopted by Calvinists and most other Protestants. The other books do occur in the Greek translation of the Old Testament and thus also in the Lutheran, Roman Catholic, and Orthodox Bibles. The difference originally had less to do with the contents than with the reading practices of the communities involved.

The average Protestant notion of the Bible concurs with the attitude that for centuries dominated scholarly circles in Western Europe, namely, *rationalism*—the view of God, humankind, and the world in which everything is connected rationally. In this view, a book is written—and, therefore, must be read—according to the conscious intention of the author. This is also true of the Bible. Everything must be read there as written according to the clear and distinct plan of God. Thus contradictions of such an approach are almost beyond description, let alone the moral shortcomings. Nonetheless, in the book of Joshua God orders Israel to eradicate all the cities of Canaan with all their inhabitants. The psalmist prays that his enemies' children be "dash[ed] . . . against the rock." Who can read such things in good faith as an expression of a clear plan of God? In this context perhaps we should reconsider the attitude toward the Jews in the New Testament. (Joshua 6:21; Psalm 137:9)

A rationalistic programming of the code word "Holy Scripture" does not work. It is better to take the Bible's function within the community as the point of departure. The Scriptures are holy because the reading community finds inspiration in them. Within the community the same is true of the reading individual. True faith feeds on personal contemplation. But this never circumvents fellowship with other believers. Time and again inspiration must be drawn from the songs and prayers of the community, from the celebration with bread and wine, from the communal reading and interpretation of Scripture. There is an intimate relationship between these writings and this reading community. That is the reason why these writings are holy. "Holy" means "set apart." These writings are set apart and read—not Plato or Shakespeare, even though their works might be more elevated in content.

When we take the individual's place within the community as the point of departure, the internal differences are no longer such a problem. Each person reads the same book in a different manner, and one book appeals to one more than the other. Justice can be done to the multifaceted nature of the Bible only within a community. It was in this manner that it emerged in the first place. The Bible is a community book to which many different groups have contributed over the course of time. To a special degree this is true of the Gospels. These are literally community texts, created within different congregations from traditions that were preserved there, and they also were made *for* those groups. Differences are then only to be expected.

Who can guarantee that the individual within the reading congregation does indeed find inspiration? No one! This is what has long been called "the work of the Holy Spirit." "Holy Spirit" is another name for God's presence. We now note that the codes are linked to one another. The code "Holy Scripture" only works together with "faith." The community of believers can *trust* that God is present and that his word indeed is heard when the Scriptures are read and explained.

Church

The code word "church" is ambiguous. On the one hand, it designates an object of faith, the "church of Christ" as an ideal. On the other, it indicates one or more concrete groups of people who at times remind one pitifully little of the gospel. When speaking of church, we must thus approach the matter both from the standpoint of faith and from the standpoint of history.

As mentioned in an earlier chapter, the word "church" is a translation of the Greek *ekklesia*. In the Greek translation of the Old Testament, the latter term indicates the gathering of the people; it is synonymous with *synagogue*. Church and synagogue are related—and not only linguistically. The customs and conventions of the church are linked by origin to those of the synagogue. I will pursue this below under the key word "liturgy." I note here, however, the churches of non-Jews came to oppose the Jews. With this, the characteristic contradiction of the later church was a fact: that of being an anti-Jewish community that preserves and develops Jewish traditions. (p. 85)

In the second century the non-Jewish church was well under way to defining its position over against Jews and pagans. This struggle was concluded in the fourth century when Emperor Constantine chose to support the church, and the status of the Jews declined rapidly. The nadir was reached in the Middle Ages in Europe. The various reformations and revolutions brought changes, especially because Christianity became divided and weakened. In modern politics—at least in Europe—Christianity no longer enjoys a privileged position compared with Judaism. Furthermore, World War II opened the eyes of many Christians to the reality of their attitude toward Jews. (chapter 1)

Thus at the beginning of the third millennium we have reached a new situation. For some time, it has not been necessary for Christians to safeguard their particular identity by opposing the Jews. On the contrary, they have discovered how great their spiritual affinity to Judaism is. Their own Christianity rests on Jewish foundations. The time has come for the church no longer to proclaim only its own message of Jesus the Christ. Alongside this it must learn to value its relationship to the Jews. A desire for improving this relationship has been expressed in an increasing number of ecclesiastical declarations from Western Europe and North America. Recent statements from the Vatican are also encouraging.

Such positive statements involve the church as an entity of faith, as an ideal. The church must learn to recognize its place alongside the synagogue before God's presence. Whatever their differences may be, in their prayers Jews and Christians stand before the same Creator and Redeemer. This means that the church acknowledges that in its confession of Jesus as Messiah it reflects only a portion of God's truth. It admits that it does not stand alone but that it needs the relationship to the synagogue. Is that not already given in the fact that this confession is contested and controverted? Is it not already given in the necessary and critical question of John the Baptist? Even the key word "church" is bound to "faith"!

An unflinching acceptance of the Jewish component in the Christian heritage can make the church more whole. Links can be recognized between seemingly disparate aspects, such as between worship and ethics, prayer and legislation, study and the love of one's neighbor. It is also possible that Roman Catholics, Protestants, and Orthodox believers can find each other anew around their rediscovered Jewish roots, and likewise Eastern and Western, evangelical and liberal Christians. Not because all that is Jewish is better, for Judaism has its negative aspects as well. Rather, the regaining of the suppressed spiritual heritage can release a new vitality.

With respect to the question of truth, the church can acknowledge its own relativity alongside that of the synagogue and can find strength while doing so. It is not necessary to be afraid of discussions and internal differences of opinion. That such is possible is shown in certain churches by an encouraging new phenomenon: the house of study. Here the intended purpose is to study the Old and New Testaments in relation to Judaism. The house of study is usually not connected to one specific church but is ecumenical. The idea emerged following the example of the "freie jüdische Lehrhaus" initiated by the Jewish thinker Franz Rosenzweig in 1920 in Frankfurt. Jews who had lost all sense of a relationship between the modern age and the Orthodox tradition found a new point of orientation there. This was picked up during and after the Second World War by Dutch and German Christians.

In this, an essential element of the church lives once more. Jesus devoted much time to teaching in the synagogue. We are told that the first church in Jerusalem "devoted themselves to the apostles' teaching." The "teaching" involves the collective studying of biblical writings, supplied where necessary with interpretation and specification. In rabbinic circles this forms a permanent part of community life. Alongside the synagogue there is, wherever possible, a "house of study." Questions from the life of the community are given ample attention. In Christian circles this was obscured. During the Middle Ages, church "doctrine" was a matter for theologians, while the people remained unenlightened. Translations of the Bible into the language of the people were a great step forward. The official church fought this tooth and nail, but the "reformation" persevered. Bible study is now fully accepted in Roman Catholic circles as well. (Matthew 4:23; Acts 2:42)

Interested readers are thus able to gather around the Bible and to inquire together concerning the meaning of what is written. In this everyone is a beginner each time, for faith must be rediscovered every day. Here, there are no stupid questions, only stupid answers—answers that do not take the question of the other seriously. Here the questions are more important than the answers, and no single answer is final. Here the point is the live discussion around the written word. Differences in viewpoints are presupposed. The rabbis relate that each word spoken from Sinai immediately had 600,000 meanings, one for each Israelite.

The house of study is situated in between the worship service and everyday life. Here the Bible is thus both "Holy Scripture" and a book beside other books. Here Plato and Shakespeare can be read alongside it, if appropriate. Here the different parts of the Bible can be read in their diversity. After all, everyone knows that later in the worship service they will be read as a unity! Here there is room for criticism of the content of certain passages, such as the destruction of cities and the dashing of children to pieces. Here there is room to speak honestly and seriously about anti-Jewish accents in the New Testament.

Liturgy

Those from Calvinist circles are not much accustomed to the code word "liturgy," although those from Eastern Orthodox, Roman Catholic, and Lutheran circles are. I refer to the worship service of the church or congregation. The Greek word originally meant "office," "public service." Of importance to us is its public nature: liturgy is service to the community. (Luke 1:23; 2 Corinthians 9:12)

Liturgy is the most public and recognizable expression of Christian faith. Practicing love for one's neighbor and standing up for freedom and justice can be that as well, just as concentrated reading of Holy Scripture and personal prayer can be, but these things can also be done in a different context: humanistic, Jewish, Islamic, etc. In contrast, the distinctive rituals of church liturgy are related to specifically Christian words and texts. The Christian quality is observable to all.

In this area the church is again closely related to the synagogue. If this seems contradictory, it is so only in appearance. Why are the characteristic parts of the Christian liturgy derived from Judaism? Because their origin lies in the circle of Jesus and his disciples.

First, three main elements are involved. I have observed that Jesus submitted to John's "baptism of repentance." I described this as an act of accepting God's kingdom, of requesting forgiveness for sins, and of resolving to do God's will. This is also the first step one can take in the church's public worship or a step that is performed for one as a child. To this is related the prayer that Jesus taught his disciples, the "Lord's Prayer," for it contains these petitions: "Your kingdom come, your will be done. . . . Forgive us our debts. . . ." This prayer was recited three times a day in the early church. The third element that goes back to Jesus and his disciples is the Eucharist, that is, the blessing of the bread and wine, which Protestants often call the "Lord's Supper." (Luke 11:2; p. 35)

These three main elements of Christian liturgy are composed entirely of Jewish components. In themselves, the words of the Lord's Prayer have nothing Christian about them. But they are unmistakably connected to Jesus. Before baptism became a Christian ritual, it had a somewhat unclear function in the Jewish repentance movement of John the Baptist. Also Jewish is the ritual of pronouncing a blessing, a *berakha* or *eucharistia* over the broken bread and the poured wine. That is precisely what Jesus' followers did—"in remembrance" of him. (1 Corinthians 11:24)

Remembrance is a key word in Jewish and Christian liturgy. During liturgical moments like the Eucharist or the Jewish Passover, important occurrences in the past are remembered, such as Jesus' last supper or the exodus of the Israelites from Egypt. The past is made present, is re-presented. There is, in fact, a relation between the two rituals. According to the first three Gospels, Jesus' last supper was a Jewish Passover meal. The Eucharist re-presents Jesus' last supper, during which he celebrated with his disciples the redemption from Egypt. The remembrance of Jesus points indirectly to the celebration of Israel's redemption.

A fourth element forms the living core of these three, the reading of Scripture. This also is derived from Judaism, which had distinguished in this respect itself from all other religions. Week by week the stories, precepts, prophecies, and songs from the Bible are heard and the congregation identifies itself with them. At times of celebration, appropriate portions are heard in which the remembrance of the past is accentuated. Before Easter, the Christian community ascends with Jesus to the festival in Jerusalem. During Easter week they remember his trial, execution, and resurrection "on the third day, in accordance with the Scriptures."

In this manner, the liturgy is a representation of the Bible in time. Through the reading of the Scriptures, the story of God with his people is re-enacted in a time-bound manner. The whole of biblical history from creation to fulfillment thus becomes a spiritual experience. In the liturgy, the Bible becomes "Holy Scripture" for the congregation, and the congregation becomes the people of the Scriptures. The New Testament does not come separately. The code word "liturgy" summarizes how it is invisibly bound to the reading community.

Central to the liturgy are the *festivals*. Two stand out: Christmas and Easter. These festivals make their influence felt far beyond the church. The rich tradition of stories and melodies has left its mark on art and music, especially in the West. Even the non-church-going European knows something about the Christmas stable and manger and about the cross at Golgotha. Public pageants of Jesus' birth and death have been performed at Christmas and Easter since the Middle Ages. Digital technology now offers broad access to classical Christmas and Easter music, such as Johann Sebastian Bach's music for the passion according to Matthew and the passion according to John.

With this we are suddenly back to the question of Jesus and the Jews. Oddly enough, the two Gospels that have had the greatest influence in the churches, as is evident from the passion music and passion plays, are the ones that exhibit the strongest anti-Jewish traits! This gives food for thought. But I am concerned here with how these Gospels are heard and could be heard within the time-bound context of the liturgy. I limit myself to John, which has the sharpest anti-Jewish features.

In an earlier chapter, I concluded that John not only reacts against Jews but also contains the rudiments of an anti-Jewish theology. At the same time, it also contains Jewish-Christian elements. This situation should not be played down to an easy "both Jewish and anti-Jewish." Taken as a whole, this Gospel is permeated with an anti-Jewish orientation, which suggests how its various parts should be read. To a large extent the same happened to the Jewish elements in the liturgy and to the entire Old Testament. It applies as well to the Gospel of Luke; although Luke emphasizes the connection to Judaism, it came to be read in an anti-Jewish manner in the anti-Jewish context of the church. (pp. 100, 110)

The structure giving coherence to the whole is decisive. Directly connected to this is the attitude of the reading community. A community that reacts against Judaism is anti-Jewish even if it appeals to elements of Jewish tradition. Could the opposite also occur? Can a community assume a position of solidarity with Jews while giving out anti-Jewish statements? This would mean that such messages contradict the actual position of the community. Such indeed is the case. In history there have been small groups of Christians who, in spite of anti-Jewish elements in their tradition, did their very best for the Jews.

Let us now imagine that a Christian congregation wants to perform the passion story of John during Lent. Assume as well that none of the members of the congregation would even think of blaming "the Jews" for Jesus' death. Imagine that their church is fittingly staged. At the climax, when Pilate has said for the third time that he finds Jesus innocent, the following words are heard: "The Jews answered him, 'We have a law, and according to that law he ought to die because he claimed to be the Son of God.'" Would this mean that the congregation, which empathizes with the story, ascribes the crucifixion to the Jews and their law? This cannot be decided directly, for personal feelings are not tangible. It would have to become apparent from the general attitude of the congregation. And what can we know of that? Furthermore, until recently such questions concerning John were not even posed! At best, the Johannine words in question sound ambiguous. (John 19:7)

It would be so much simpler and more consistent if this congregation were to perform the passion story of Luke. The distress about the unjust suffering of Jesus and the desire not to abandon him are certainly not less. Not "the Jews" but the chief priests and their followers are the ones who let Jesus be crucified there. The Pharisees are not drawn into the story. "A great number of the people" accompanied Jesus to the place of execution. The intimate bond with his people is embodied in the mourning women. Jesus turned around and said, "Daughters of Jerusalem, do not weep for me, but weep for yourselves and your children. For the days are surely coming when they will say, 'Blessed are the barren, and the wombs that never bore, and the breasts that never nursed.'... For if they do this when the wood is green, what will happen when it is dry?" How naturally could the congregation connect its grief and anger concerning Jesus' death with its sympathy for the Jewish people by siding with these Jewish women through the representation in the liturgy! (Luke 23:27)

Here lies the problem. In the liturgy, the church reads the New Testament as a unity. But what unity is there between Luke and John? Must we read Luke from the anti-Jewish perspective of John? That is what has been done in church history, but must it remain so? Does a Christian congregation not have the right to seek unity in the New Testament by turning things around? Luke has a legitimate place in the canon. May the congregation not rather read John from the perspective of Luke, where the bond with the Jews is emphasized?

To this end, such a congregation could clarify its own position toward the Jews in various ways. Encounters with Jews in the context of a house of study could be helpful. The congregation could also explicitly distance itself from the anti-Jewish orientation voiced in John. This could be done by a few words that show identification with the community that finds expression in Luke.

Taking one's distance from the Gospel of John does not mean that this Gospel is written off. On the contrary, it too remains a text of the church, a text full of pain and hate. The Gospel as we have it shows clear traces of a conflict with the local synagogue. In no other text are the pain and hostility so tangible. The wounds are, as it were, still fresh. John is the Gospel of a traumatized congregation.

This insight opens new possibilities for treating the Gospel of John. We can embrace it as a precious document of the church in one of her most difficult moments. The pressure of those circumstances, however, led also to a position on the Jews that conflicts with the fundamental position of the church. This Johannine stance is the anti-Jewish position that became dominant in the later church. As such, John became a characteristic and "familiar" Gospel.

This image of the Gospel of John as a document of a traumatized anti-Jewish church can be depicted in the liturgy. The congregation can give it dramatic form by stating, "This, too, is our Gospel," thereby giving the inherited anti-Judaism a place. Without supressing it, we can dissociate ourselves from its anti-Judaism. Thus also, without ambivalence or misunderstanding, justice can ultimately be done to the profound beauty of this Gospel.

Gospel

The final code word brings us back to the beginning, to Jesus' own message. "Gospel" is a heavily loaded word. Not only is it considered to be the hallmark of the church and "preaching the gospel" taken to mean "persuading people to join the church," but it is also used as a characteristic of "evangelical" politics and as a designation of groups who consider "Christian" to be too vague. There is no need to doubt the integrity of the motives behind these. The point is that "gospel" is reduced to the programs or ideologies of action groups both within and outside of the church.

It is even questionable to what extent we can equate "gospel" with the *Christian* message. Jesus was not a Christian but a Jew. His message was not intended for "evangelicals" or "Christians," but for what he called "the lost sheep of the house of Israel." These were human beings without hope of redemption or healing, those cast out or disdained, people who could not bear the evil of this world. Among Jesus' words, "beatitudes" have been passed down. In these words of encouragement and comfort, he addresses the "poor in Spirit," "those who mourn," and "the meek"; "those who hunger and thirst for righteousness" and who are "merciful," "pure of heart," and "peacemakers." In the oldest report, Mark, Jesus' message is called "the good news [gospel] of God." (Matthew 15:24; 5:3; Mark 1:14; pp. 36, 37)

"Gospel" means originally "good news for the poor." We saw that the word is rooted in Isaiah's message of God's hopeful future for Israel and the nations. The "gospel of Jesus" linked up with the words of Isaiah. Along with many other Jews of his day, each time he read these words full of expectation. Paul speaks of "the gospel of Christ" and often means "the good news *about* Jesus." But he also speaks of "the gospel of God, which he promised beforehand through his prophets . . . concerning his Son. . . ." He, too, intends something broad: "the gospel of God" that is linked to the words of the prophets and to the message of Jesus himself. (Galatians 1:7; Romans 1:16; 15:16)

Too often, "gospel" is narrowed to the proclamation of "the Christ of faith," to a summarization of Jesus' theological significance. It involves labels such as "Christ," "Lord," and "Son of God." The importance of this is obvious. In the tradition of Jesus' words, however, other standards hold: "Not everyone who says to me, 'Lord, Lord' will enter the kingdom of heaven, but only the one who *does* the will of my Father in heaven. . . . Everyone then who hears these words of mine *and acts on them* will be like a wise man who built his house on rock. . . . And everyone who hears these words of mine and does not act on them will be like a foolish man who built his house on sand. . . ." Another tradition also expresses the breadth of Jesus' message, for example, showing that it goes beyond the limitations of family relations: "Who are my mother and my brothers? . . . Whoever *does* the will of God is my brother and sister and mother." That God's will must be *done* is also underscored in the Lord's Prayer: " . . . *on earth*, as it is in heaven." (Matthew 7:21; Mark 3:33)

It is easy to argue that the church and Christianity do not actualize "the gospel of Jesus." But do we have the right to speak here if we do not take upon ourselves the specific standards of Jesus' message?

"Church" is an ambiguous concept, as I have said. On the one hand, it is an ideal and, on the other, a human movement with inevitable shortcomings. The church's greatest problem is that it, too, is composed of people. There are many outside of the church who love their neighbor as Jesus intended, who thirst for justice, and who strive for peace. That is true, and we should welcome them. But where is Jesus' memory kept alive and his "gospel" recognizably witnessed if not in that problematic community of humans, the church?

The gospel itself is not available separately. It presumes "faith" that embraces doubt, a reading community with its "holy scripture," a "church" that recognizes itself as having a place beside Israel, and a "liturgy" that keeps the remembrance of Jesus alive among his people. The gospel presupposes readers who activate these code words.

Appendix

Jewish Movements in the Time of Jesus

I discussed on pages 28–32 the various movements in the Jewish homeland at the time of Jesus. They were distinguished by their specific understanding of the law of Moses and their practice of the commandments. The Pharisees were divided into the schools of Shammai and Hillel.

For the purposes of this book it is important to be able to place the Jesus movement within that whole. We know but little about this movement, and we are unable to determine exactly what Jesus himself taught, what he adopted from others, and what was later ascribed to him. We are able, however, to speak of Jesus' milieu.

In the chart on p. 139, I indicate basic tendencies of the known groups. In addition, on matters of Sabbath and purity we are able to distinguish between a conservative and a more innovative attitude. The importance of the belief in angels and the resurrection of the dead is emphasized particularly in the New Testament.

This survey is a reconstruction on the basis of various available sources. Documentation can be found in the passages below, among other places. For historical reconstruction, information from the various sources must, of course, be considered.

	Sabbath	purity	marriage, divorce	non-Jews	angels, resurrection
Sadducees	strict, conservative	not strict, conservative	?	?	reject the ideas
Essenes	very strict, conservative	very strict, conservative	very strict	closed	strong belief
Pharisees, Shammaites	fairly strict, conservative	less strict, conservative	fairly strict	fairly closed	strong belief
Pharisees, Hillelites	flexible, innovative	fairly strict, innovative	flexible	open	moderate belief
milieu of Jesus	flexible, innovative	not strict, conservative	very strict	fairly closed/ open	strong belief

Flavius Josephus

Essenes, Sadducees, Pharisees: *The Jewish War* 2:119–166; *Jewish Antiquities* 13:171–173; 18:11-22.

Jesus' milieu: *Jewish Antiquities* 18:116–119; 20:200–201.

Qumran

Essenes: *Community Rule* = 1QS 3:13—5:26; 6:13–23; *Damascus Document*= CD 10:10—11:18.

Essenes, Pharisees (?): Halakic letter = 4QMMTb 3–5; 63–66.

Rabbinic Literature

Shammaites, Hillelites: Mishnah, *Shabbat* 1:4–7; *Gittin* 9:10; *Hullin* 2:7; *Yadayim* 3:1-2; Tosefta, *Pesahim* 1:7; *Shekalim* 3:16; *Sanhedrin* 13:1–5.

Pharisees, Sadducees: Mishnah, *Sanhedrin* 10:1; *Yadayim* 4:6-7.

New Testament

Sadducees, Pharisees, Jesus' milieu: Acts of the Apostles 4:1-7; 5:17-40; 22:30—23:10.

Pharisees, Jesus' milieu: Luke 6:1-11; 11:37-44; Mark 10:2-12.

Sadducees, Jesus' milieu: Mark 12:18-27.

Index of Names and Subjects

Index of Ancient Sources